Steps Academics Can Take Now to Protect and Grow Their Portfolios

Tony W. Sigmon, PhD, MBA

iUniverse, Inc.
New York Bloomington

Steps Academics Can Take Now to Protect and Grow Their Portfolios

iUniverse books may be ordered through booksellers or by contacting:

iUniverse
1663 Liberty Drive
Bloomington, IN 47403
www.iuniverse.com
1-800-Authors (1-800-288-4677)

Because of the dynamic nature of the Internet, any Web addresses or links contained in this book may have changed since publication and may no longer be valid. The views expressed in this work are solely those of the author and do not necessarily reflect the views of the publisher, and the publisher hereby disclaims any responsibility for them.

ISBN: 978-1-4401-5404-1 (sc)
ISBN: 978-1-4401-5403-4 (dj)
ISBN: 978-1-4401-5405-8 (ebk)

Printed in the United States of America

iUniverse rev. date: 6/26/2009

Preface

This book provides university faculty and staff with an overview of several key investment strategies developed by our firm. These approaches have been tested and proven successful in helping our clients achieve their retirement goals.

We address those factors that affect the academic's ability to attain his or her investment goals, identify the universe of investment options, explore the constraints and flexibilities inherent in university-sponsored retirement plans, and describe philosophies for managing retirement portfolios. Specific, real-life case studies help guide readers in applying various concepts to their individual circumstances. Although we have attempted to address a wide range of investor challenges, the infinite combination of potential market conditions and individual circumstances prevent us from suggesting approaches for all possibilities.

The book also provides a rationale for taking a comprehensive approach to asset management that treats all investor accounts as a single collective portfolio. Approaches are described that can be used to bring together these accounts under tactical unified management that is free of vendor bias.

Because of the intrinsic differences between public and private university retirement plans, certain generalizations have been made when discussing various retirement plan issues. However, the concepts described are applicable to academics at both public and private institutions.

Some of the concepts presented have tax implications. We advise individuals to discuss tax issues with an accountant to ensure that any actions that may be taken as a result of information presented in this book are consistent with tax law and carried out in the individual's best interest.

Table of Contents

List of Case Studies

List of Figures

List of Tables

Chapter 1

Introduction

The Financial Markets

Financial markets are rarely predictable beasts. Both the U.S. and foreign stock markets began a decline at the turn of the century, persisted through the tragedy of 9-11-2001, and continued to struggle through 2002. These markets then began a climb until 2007, at which point they began a historic tumble that saw them lose about 40 percent of their value.

This unpredictability creates concerns for all investors and has caused extra consternation for those individuals who rely on equities for a portion of their retirement savings. In good times it is difficult to realize that things can be bad. In bad times it is equally difficult, if not more so, to realize that things will be good again. However, history tells us that every downturn is followed by an upturn.

Investors have many means of positioning their portfolios for participating effectively in recovery cycles and blunting the impact of downturns. Staying on top of one's financial picture, in good times and bad, is critical. Especially during periods of poor stock performance and early recovery, we have to open our statements, take stock of our positions, and reestablish not just our goals, but the best path to reach them. Many academics have the ability to do more than they realize to improve efficiency and create solid footing no matter the state of the equity markets.

About Our Firm

As you progress through this book, it should be clear to you that managing university-based retirement portfolios is a complex process requiring informed decisions, strategic planning, and continual reevaluation of these plans so that the assets you accumulate during your working years support the retirement you hope for.

Collegiate Capital Management was founded in 1994, and has served hundreds of university faculty and staff throughout the United States. In our experience, few university employees have the detailed knowledge or the time to structure and manage their retirement assets effectively. The focus of our business is to provide these services to academics and university staff. Our expertise enables our clients to move confidently toward retirement, knowing that the concepts presented in this book help them to create significantly more value in their investment accounts than they could on their own.

Collegiate Capital Management is a **registered investment advisory** firm that is regulated by the Securities and Exchange Commission (SEC). Since its inception in 1994, the firm's principals have provided **investment advisory services** for both retirement assets and **after-tax assets** for individuals, trusts, endowments, and college savings plans. The firm has offices in North Carolina and Georgia and serves clients throughout the United States as well as other countries.

> **Registered investment advisory:** A firm that manages the investments of others. The firm is regulated by the firm's state of residency or the Securities and Exchange Commission, depending on the level of assets under management.
>
> **Investment advisory services:** The development and implementation of individual investment plans along with the ongoing supervisory management of investment assets according to this plan.
>
> **After-tax assets:** Assets for which ordinary income taxes have been previously paid.

The firm's advisors have a depth of understanding of **university-sponsored retirement plans** available to university faculty and staff, a breadth of understanding of the financial markets, and an innovative approach to asset management. Together, these attributes offer our clients an exceptional blend of capabilities that have proven to be valuable resources for our clients.

> **University-sponsored retirement plan:** A retirement plan established by a university employer that stipulates the conditions for participation by employees, such as vendor availability, annual contribution limit, and withdrawal restrictions.

Over the years, we have recruited a group of highly trained and dedicated investment advisor representatives and support staff to serve our clients. The firm's staff consists of individuals who are educated in finance, management information systems, the physical sciences, engineering, and mathematics. Our investment professionals are investment advisor representatives of Collegiate Capital Management and therefore are regulated by the SEC. These individuals are also securities representatives licensed and regulated by the Financial Industry Regulatory Authority (FINRA).

Since representatives of our firm are not agents of any investment provider, our advice is not driven by compensation from any financial entity. This allows our advisors to provide our clients with unbiased recommendations based solely on decisions that are in our clients' best interest. Our representatives also operate differently from **stockbrokers,** who receive commissions based upon transactions, rarely understand university retirement plans in detail, and in many cases are not licensed investment advisor representatives able to legally provide ongoing investment advice for university retirement accounts. Our firm is not driven by commissions but simply by those actions that are in our clients' best interests.

> Stockbroker: A regulated professional who buys and sells securities based upon a client's instructions and generally receives a commission for completing the transaction.

For the same reason that portfolios should be free of broker commission, investors should receive independent counsel that is free of **vendor** bias. Representatives of a particular vendor have an allegiance to their employer. These representatives often suggest that their product's limited investment offerings are sufficient for your needs or are the most appropriate for a wide range of accounts. This advice could be driven by an anticipation of commissions or the inherent conflict between the interests of the client and that of the representative's employer. Our clients know that our advice is provided in an environment free of conflicts of interest with any vendor in their university retirement plans. It is imperative that your portfolio be structured in a manner that efficiently utilizes the strengths of each vendor's product. Only an approach that considers all of the investment options in a university plan makes this possible.

> Vendor: A company that participates in a university's retirement plan by accepting employer and employee contributions and offering various investment options to a participant.

Investors sometimes use an investment firm to manage their non-university accounts and allow their university-sponsored retirement plan to go without ongoing management or seek the occasional advice of a vendor's representative for these latter assets. Our firm's thorough knowledge of the many different investment accounts available to our clients allows us to provide a cohesive approach to asset management. An investment professional without this comprehensive knowledge is not able to provide this same type of integrated approach. The outcome is a structuring of individual **accounts** into **portfolios** that mitigate the redundancy that may occur when accounts are invested with no unified management strategy.

> <u>Account:</u> A vehicle that allows for investing, including the purchase, sale, and holding of assets with a given vendor.
>
> <u>Portfolio:</u> The collection of accounts that encompasses all of your invested assets.

Creating Flexibility With Your Investment Accounts

This book is intended to provide university faculty and staff with information that can be used to improve the flexibility and efficiency of their investment portfolios by introducing concepts that we have used with our clients for over 15 years. As we will describe in more detail later, those with **retirement assets** accumulated while working at previous employers or who have attained a certain age are presented with opportunities that can enhance their portfolios. The opportunities offered by these **triggering events** can help you complement the limited options available in most **mandatory retirement plans** by allowing access to less volatile and less risky **fixed-income investments** that are not available in university retirement accounts. These opportunities can also provide for a wider complement of **equity-based investments** than those offered within restrictive university-sponsored plans. The more weapons at your disposal, the more likely your chances of success.

<u>Retirement assets</u>: Assets that are anticipated to be used to produce retirement income.

<u>Triggering event</u>: A milestone that a participant experiences in order to become eligible to receive a distribution from a retirement plan.

<u>Mandatory retirement plans</u>: A retirement account for which participation is a condition of employment.

<u>Fixed-income investments</u>: Bonds, money market funds, fixed annuities, and stable value funds that pay a specific rate of interest.

<u>Equity-based investments</u>: Funds invested primarily in common or preferred stock of a company.

Many academics are not aware of the opportunities available to them with their retirement savings. Throughout this book, we will look at those opportunities, discuss how to take advantage of them, and explore the benefits they hold. This book will bring you up to speed on these many unknowns and help you maximize the promise of your retirement. We discuss later the various financial risks associated with investing. These can be dwarfed by the risk associated with lack of or the ill-informed management of your assets. In short, with respect to university retirement accounts, you may not know what you don't know.

The Busy and Stressful Life of the Academic

The academic life is filled with responsibilities — from teaching, conducting research, publishing, advising, and managing administrative tasks to addressing family and other personal issues. Among these responsibilities and the relaxation we all need, you must make decisions that will influence whether you will reach your retirement goals. Proper management of your retirement portfolio requires an ongoing effort. Many academics simply do not have the time, inclination, or resources to properly manage this complex component of their lives.

A young faculty member hired into her first position suddenly finds herself in a whirlwind of activity. After moving her family to a new city, preparing class notes, perhaps setting up a laboratory, and completing all the other day-to-day tasks required by the move, she must pick a retirement plan and a vendor within that plan. In many cases, people do this without the time for a thoughtful decision. Often, faculty members make selections based on decisions their colleagues may have previously made or based on the name of a vendor alone, without conducting the analysis that the decision deserves.

Worse, in many cases, the decision is never revisited, especially when the economy is strong. This process continues as an individual moves to positions with other universities. What results is a preponderance of individuals selecting the same vendor without conducting their own due diligence regarding the performance and other characteristics of the investment options the vendor provides. To compound this problem, it is not unusual for these accounts to be ignored for decades, without meaningful analysis or reevaluation of the original investment options or the alternatives that become available. People sometimes follow this course even in the face of major changes in retirement plans that might add or delete vendors or investment options from their past and present employers' plans.

Without proper, ongoing attention to your investment accounts, you could be exposing yourself to **credit, market, longevity,** and **inflation risks** that could hinder your ability to reach your retirement goals.

> Credit risk: Risk of loss of principal due to the default of the issuer.
>
> Market risk: Risk of loss due to a decline in the overall market.
>
> Longevity risk: Risk that you and/or your spouse may outlive your assets.
>
> Inflation risk: Risk that your assets will not grow at a rate sufficient to maintain purchasing power.

Case Studies

Case Study 1: Not Getting Unbiased Objective Information Can Be Costly

Scenario: Edith is a sociologist and has worked with her current university employer for 15 years. This was her first academic position. When she was initially hired, she took the advice of a colleague in selecting a mandatory retirement plan vendor and the advice of a phone representative of the vendor in selecting her investment options. She has been busy, feels overwhelmed with information, and really doesn't understand her options, so she has never revisited her selections or evaluated them against other options her employer offers.

Solution: Edith decided to discuss her situation with an independent advisor who doesn't have the biases of a university vendor. Edith met with her advisor and found out that she did not have the proper allocation of her assets for her age and risk profile. In addition, she learned that several of the investments she was holding had been underperformers compared to other options available to her. The advisor suggested changes that would enhance her allocation and place her in investments with a better performance history.

Case Study 2: Your Accounts Should Be Managed as a Cohesive Portfolio

Scenario: Archie has had positions with two universities over the last 20 years. He has retirement accounts from both of those positions. In addition to these accounts, his wife has an employer-sponsored plan, and they have an additional investment account that they own jointly. Archie and his wife are using a local stockbroker to manage the jointly owned account, while the employer-sponsored accounts are running on autopilot with little attention having been given to them. The stockbroker seems to not really be aware of the employer-sponsored plans, since he has never asked how those accounts are invested or has given them only a cursory nod.

Solution: Archie should find an investment professional who understands how to integrate all these accounts into one cohesive portfolio. Chances are, there is considerable redundancy in his investments, significant investment types have been completely ignored, and changes have been made in his employer-sponsored plans that could be used to his advantage.

Case Study 3: Don't Assume Vendors Are Managing Your Accounts

Scenario: Gloria has had two university employers. She was a faculty member for 15 years with a university in Arizona and has been at her current university for the past 12 years. All her assets are with a single vendor, and the assets in each employer account are invested in the same three mutual funds. Gloria is under the mistaken impression that since the funds in which she is invested are managed by the vendor she has selected, the allocation of her assets across investment types is also being actively managed by the vendor she is using.

Solution: Only a registered investment advisor representative can actively manage investment assets. Representatives of a vendor can offer suggestions, but they must take investment instructions from the investor and can't make any changes unless these instructions are given. Vendor representatives by federal regulation may only discuss their own product offerings. They are simply not allowed to give advice that includes options offered by other vendors. Gloria should change her approach by taking a more active role in the management of her accounts or by enlisting the assistance of an independent advisor professional to do this for her.

Chapter 2

Characteristics of University-Sponsored Retirement Plans

University-sponsored retirement plans are governed by IRS regulations, state statutes, and restrictions established by each university or university system. Many of these plans have come to be known by the section of the IRS code that governs participation in the plan. Two types of plans are available: 1) those that are required as a condition of employment; and 2) those in which participation is a prerogative of the employee.

University-Sponsored Mandatory Retirement Plans

Participation in a mandatory retirement plan is the cornerstone for attaining retirement goals. The university requires participation in this plan as a necessary condition for employment, and the university or a related entity acts as the **plan sponsor**.

Plan sponsor: An organization or entity that offers a retirement plan to an employee group. In the case of a plan maintained by a single employer, the plan sponsor is generally the employer. In the case of a plan maintained by one or more employers or organizations, the plan sponsor is the association, committee, joint board of trustees or other similar group of representatives of the parties involved.

In most cases, both employer and employee contributions are made to the mandatory plan, with employee contributions made through payroll deduction. The rates of employer and employee contribution are established by state statute in the case of public universities or by the university itself, in the case of private universities. In either instance, the IRS requires that the university establish, maintain, and adhere to a **plan document** for any mandatory plan.

Plan document: The document that describes the various rules which govern an employer-sponsored retirement plan. This document is created and, when necessary, amended by the plan sponsor.

Generally, both university and employee contributions are made to the mandatory plan based on a percentage of the employee's salary. Employer contributions are an expense of the university and are not considered income to the employee at the time the contributions are made. Therefore, these contributions, as well as any earnings, are taxed as income when taxable **distributions** are taken. Employee contributions to a mandatory plan are treated as **before-tax contributions** and are taxed only when they are distributed.

Distributions: The payment of funds from a retirement or pension plan.

Before-tax contributions: The portion of an employee's salary contributed to a retirement plan before federal income taxes are deducted, resulting in a reduction in the individual's gross income for federal and state tax purposes.

Public and private universities may differ in the types of mandatory retirement plans they offer to employees. Public universities generally, but not always, offer both a **defined benefit (DB) retirement plan** and a **defined contribution (DC) retirement plan**.

> Defined benefit retirement plan: Retirement plan for which the benefits are based on years of service, salary, actuarial factors, and income payment option selected. These are sometimes called pensions and require little employee involvement until retirement, when the retiree determines how he or she would like to receive disbursement.
>
> Defined contribution retirement plan: Retirement plan for which the retirement benefit (i.e., the payout) will depend on several factors including how well the investments have performed over time, age at retirement, and cumulative amount of contributions.

At many public universities, faculty members and those in certain administrative positions have a choice between these two plans. At others, all employees can choose between these two options. There is no single "best" option between these two plans. The choice is very much an individual one, in which many factors should be taken into account, such as a person's aversion to risk, vesting differences between the plans, an individual's anticipated length of employment with the current employer, other retirement assets, and other financial and personal considerations. Over the years, the term Optional Retirement Plan (ORP) has come to be used in reference to the mandatory DC plan in many public universities. It's a confusing term because the word "optional" is meant to imply the option between the defined benefit and defined contribution mandatory plans. In a vast majority of large private universities, the only mandatory plan is a defined contribution plan. In the remainder of the book, a reference to the ORP should be understood to be a reference to a university's mandatory retirement plan, regardless of whether the university is public or private.

For defined contribution plans, the plan sponsor selects the vendors that are allowed in the plan and must in turn approve the various investment options offered by each vendor. Employees who choose a defined contribution plan must also choose one or more vendors to receive their contributions each payroll period. Employees then establish an account with their vendor(s) and select the investment options for their contributions.

The employee's salary determines the maximum amount of combined employer and employee contributions that can be made to a mandatory defined contribution plan. For calendar year 2009, IRS regulations limit contributions to defined contribution plans to those based upon gross salaries of up to $245,000.

Defined benefit plan assets are managed as a pooled account in which all participant assets are commingled. Once a decision is made to participate in a defined benefit plan, the employee has limited involvement until her retirement, when decisions must be made as to the manner in which she will receive her benefit as retirement income.

Additional Savings With Supplemental Retirement Plans

Supplemental retirement plans are available for retirement savings over and above participation in mandatory plans. Most supplemental retirement plans contain only employee contributions, although some private universities do make employer contributions to these plans. These plans can play an important role in attaining your retirement goals by allowing you to increase your savings and by expanding the investment options available beyond those offered in mandatory plans. Because supplemental plans are university-sponsored, contributions to these plans must be made through a payroll deduction in the same manner as those made to mandatory plans.

> Supplemental retirement plan: A voluntary plan that allows employees to make contributions, over and above mandatory contributions, via payroll deductions; these include 403(b), 401(k), and 457(b) plans.

Contributions to supplemental retirement plans have historically been made on a before-tax basis. At public universities, mandatory and supplemental plans are distinct, stand-alone accounts. At private universities, these two plans are in some cases governed by a consolidated plan document. In this case, a single account may contain both the mandatory and supplemental contributions plus earnings. The vendor then has the responsibility for maintaining proper accounting to distinguish the various contribution types.

University employers offer up to three supplemental retirement plans, generally referred to by the section of the IRS code that establishes the rules that define each. Supplemental plans available to university employees may include the following:

> ➤ 403(b): Also in the past has been referred to as a tax-sheltered annuity plan. These plans are available only to certain employees of educational and other tax-exempt organizations.
> ➤ 401(k): Similar in many respects to 403(b) plans. These plans however are not exclusive to educational and tax-exempt organizations.
> ➤ 457(b): Tax-deferred plan that can be offered by public and private organizations. The rules that govern 457(b) plans for public organizations make these plans similar in many respects to 403(b) and 401(k) plans. One of the primary distinguishing characteristics of 457(b) plans are the rules that govern withdrawals. The IRS allows withdrawals before age 59 ½ without the normal 10 percent early withdrawal penalty imposed on retirement accounts if the investor has terminated employment with the sponsoring employer.

Mandatory DC plans are generally 401(a), 403(a), or 403(b) plans as well. However, the rules that define these mandatory plans are distinct from those that govern supplemental plans defined under these same sections of the IRS code.

Supplemental plan contribution limits for 2009 are shown in Table 1. The IRS allows all university employees to contribute 100 percent of taxable income up to $16,500 per year into 401(k), 403(b), and 457(b) plans. For those who are at least 50 years old in 2009, an additional $5,500 can be contributed. Contributions made to 403(b) and 401(k) plans are aggregated. This aggregated sum cannot exceed the single plan annual contribution limit allowed. For example, someone who is less than 50 years old and contributes $1,000 to a 401(k) plan is then limited to contributing a total of $15,500 to a 403(b) plan.

Table 1 – Supplemental Retirement Plan Contribution Limits for 2009

Account	General Limit	Catch-Up*	Total
403(b)	$16,500	$5,500	$22,000
401(k)	$16,500	$5,500	$22,000
457(b)	$16,500	$5,500	$22,000

* Additional contribution amount allowable for those 50 years and older.
Source: Internal Revenue Code

Subject to the above constraint, the contributions to the 403(b) and/or 401(k) plans and those made to 457(b) plans are additive. Annual contributions to 401(k) and/or 403(b) plans do not affect the allowable contributions to a 457(b) plan for that year. For example, for someone younger than 50 years old, $16,500 can be contributed to a 403(b) plan and the same amount can be contributed to a 457(b) plan. For those who are older than 50 or will attain the age of 50 in the current year, $22,000 can be contributed to the combination of 401(k) and 403(b) plans and an additional $22,000 to a 457(b) plan.

The IRS also limits the annual contributions to all mandatory and supplemental defined contribution plans combined. This limit for 2009 is $49,000 for those younger than 50 years old and $54,500 for those individuals who will be at least 50 years old in 2009. Since a 457(b) plan is a deferred compensation plan, contributions to a 457(b) are not included in the overall limit on contributions to all DC plans.

The IRS also allows a special catch-up in deferred compensation plans for individuals within three years of retirement. These individuals are allowed to contribute as much as twice the general limit in the three years prior to the year of their retirement if they have under-contributed to their 457(b) with their current employer in previous years. Therefore, those individuals, in addition to contributions made to supplemental 403(b) and 401(k) plans, can contribute up to an additional $33,000 to a 457(b) plan.

Generally, contributions to supplemental plans are treated as before-tax contributions. So if, for example, an individual is in the 25% federal and 6% state tax brackets, a $1,000 contribution would result in a net decrease of $690 per month in take-home pay. These contributions, plus any earnings, are then taxed when funds are withdrawn from the account.

Constantly Changing IRS Regulations

IRS rules that define various aspects of university retirement plans are constantly under review and changing over time. These rules establish, among other things, the annual contribution limits shown in Table 1, the responsibilities of the plan sponsor, and various additional factors that govern participation in the plan. Supplemental 403(b) plans in particular have undergone a major restructuring over the last three years. IRS regulations have attempted to impose on these plans many of the regulations that have historically been associated with 401(k) plans. In large part, these new 403(b) rules grant or impose on the employer a higher level of **fiduciary** responsibility.

> **Fiduciary:** A person who is vested with legal rights and powers to be exercised for the benefit of another person.

These new rules require that a plan document be in place that governs various aspects of participation in the plan including eligibility to participate, allowable vendors and investment options, participant loan privileges, and the ability to make hardship withdrawals from the plan. Additionally, new IRS rules allow participants in 403(b) and 401(k) plans to designate all or a portion of their contributions to be **after-tax contributions** to a Roth 403(b) or 401(k) account. The vendor has the responsibility to maintain records that allocate contributions and subsequent earnings between these two contribution types.

> **After-tax contributions:** Monies contributed to an account on which taxes have previously been paid.

IRS regulations have historically constrained the investment options available in 403(b) plans to **mutual funds** and **annuities**. Generally, universities and/or state governments have imposed these same restrictions on 401(k) and 457(b) plans. New rules governing 403(b) plans have extended the allowable investment options for 403(b) plans to include **exchange traded funds** (ETF). The availability of ETFs in these plans is, however, at the discretion of the employer.

> <u>Mutual fund</u>: A fund operated by an investment company that invests in one or more categories of assets, including stocks, bonds, real estate, commodities, money market instruments, etc.
>
> <u>Annuities</u>: Investment contracts offered by life insurance companies that provide tax deferral of earnings. Annuities are sold in units, not shares. Annuity contracts have two phases, the accumulation phase (deferred contract) and the payout phase (annuitized contract). Most deferred contracts allow flexible distributions. If annuitized, contracts set forth the terms of paying out the proceeds of the contract with little, if any, flexibility after the initiation of payments.
>
> <u>Exchange traded fund</u>: A collection of assets such as stocks and bonds that trade continuously during the day in the same manner as individual stocks. These instruments are usually designed to track some broad market, industry, or commodity specific index.

Universities generally further limit the mutual fund and annuity options offered in defined contribution and deferred compensation plans to a small number of mutual fund and annuity vendors. Each of these vendors, in turn, offers to participants a limited number of investment options that are subject to review and approval by the plan sponsor.

Many university employees have previously invested in variable annuities within their 403(b) accounts. These investment products are an artifact of the pre-1974 IRS code regulations that only allowed annuities issued by insurance companies. Hence the out-of-date use of the terms "tax sheltered annuity" or "tax-deferred annuity" for 403(b) accounts. The 1974 legislation permitted contributions to 403(b) plans to be invested in mutual funds. Universities were slow to adapt to this change, which has resulted in a preponderance of annuities in older individual 403(b) accounts.

The individual investment options within variable annuities are referred to as **subaccounts.** In many cases, annuity products also have additional expenses over and above the **management expenses** associated with the subaccounts.

> <u>Subaccount</u>: The various investment options within an annuity product.
>
> <u>Management expense</u>: A charge paid to a mutual fund's investment adviser for its services. The annual fee is disclosed in each fund prospectus and is typically between 0.5 percent and 2.5 precent.

These extra expenses include a mortality expense to cover the potential loss on guaranteed lifetime payments and additional administrative expenses. These revenue streams are designed to provide a reserve for the insurance company in case of loss on guaranteed payout contracts, such as lifetime annuitizations.

Annuities can be purchased in retirement accounts such as 403(b) plans or as after-tax investments. Since annuities are insurance products, any tax on earnings in after-tax annuities is deferred until distributions are taken. However, the taxes on earnings in retirement accounts are automatically deferred until distributions are taken. So the added expenses associated with annuities are somewhat counterbalanced by the tax deferral benefits of after-tax annuities. However, it can be argued that the additional annuity expenses do not provide any added benefit that would not automatically be available in retirement accounts. For these reasons, investors should carefully weigh the pros and cons of investment in annuities in 403(b) accounts, or for that matter in any retirement account. University employers are now beginning to realize that investment in annuities may not be in the best interest of their employees and are beginning to move away from offering these products in 403(b) plans.

Case Studies

Case Study 1: It May Make Sense to Take the Pension From a Previous Employer Before You Retire

Scenario: Kramer is 55, has been with his current university employer for 10 years, and has a DB pension plan from a previous employer. He is eligible to begin pension payments because of his age and years of service with this previous employer but does not need the extra income. His benefit will be $1,500 per month and, except for a cost of living increase, which he would receive even if he began receiving payments now, there is no benefit to waiting until after he retires to begin receiving these payments. He is hesitant to take the pension now since he knows he will have to pay income taxes on these payments. He is currently contributing the maximum amount to his 403(b) plan.

Solution: There is no advantage for Kramer to wait until retirement to begin receiving his retirement benefit from his previous employer, so he should begin receiving those pension payments now. To defer payment of income tax, he can simply open a 457(b) account and contribute $1,500 per month to that plan from his paycheck. The $1,500 pension payment can then be used to offset the reduction in his paycheck resulting from his contribution to the 457(b) plan. Kramer should instruct his previous employer to withhold taxes on his pension since the increased payroll contribution will result in a reduction in the amount of taxes withheld from his paycheck by his current employer.

Case Study 2: Consider Starting Your Social Security Benefit Even While Still Working

Scenario: Elaine is at her social security full retirement age of 66 years and 6 months, loves her job, and wants to keep working for two more years. Her monthly benefit would be $2,000 per month if she began receiving her social security payments now. Elaine knows that if she waits until she retires to begin receiving her social security benefit, she will receive a larger monthly payment. She is also aware that if she begins receiving social security payments now, her income from the university would result in 85% of this benefit being subject to income taxes. She has convinced herself that the additional income she would receive from social security after two years does not justify her forgoing the two years of social security benefit she could receive during the last two years of employment. She just can't stomach having to pay taxes on the social benefit she would receive while working for two more years. She does not currently contribute to any supplemental retirement plan.

Solution: Elaine's solution is basically the same as Kramer's. Taxes on her $24,000 annual social security benefit can be deferred by contributing that amount to supplemental plans at the university. Since only 85 percent of her total benefit would be subject to income tax, she could defer taxes on this by contributing $20,400 (85 percent of $24,000) to her 403(b) account. Her taxable income will not change since she has offset her taxable social security benefit by contributing the same amount to her before-tax supplemental retirement plans. Elaine should instruct her employer to increase the rate of tax withholding from her check to offset the reduction in taxes withheld because of the supplemental plan contributions she will me making.

Case Study 3: University Retirement Plans Can Be Used to Defer Taxes on Outside Sources of Income

Scenario: Jerry is a 47-year old engineering professor who performs consulting work for a few different clients each year. His consulting income is usually around $10,000 per year, but in a good year he can receive as much as $20,000 from his consulting work. The IRS allows him to open an individual retirement account for his consulting business, but IRS rules will not allow him to contribute more than 25 percent of his consulting income to such a plan. This would limit him to contributing $2,500 to the retirement plan of his consulting business in a normal year and $5,000 in a good year. He would like to defer taxes on all his consulting income. He generally contributes about $10,000 per year to a supplemental 403(b) plan.

Solution: As in the case of Kramer and Elaine, Jerry's solution lies in his access to his university-sponsored supplemental retirement plans. Because of his age, Jerry can contribute $16,500 to a 403(b) plan and the same amount to a 457(b) plan — a total of $33,000. Since he can contribute as much as $23,000 more to his supplemental plans at the university, he would be able to defer taxes on all of his consulting income, even in a good year.

Case Study 4: Are You Getting Consistent Information From Vendor Representatives

Scenario: George has been with his current university employer for 25 years. He has diligently contributed annually to a 403(b) account for 20 years and has built up a nice supplement to his mandatory retirement plan. A representative of an annuity vendor helped him open the account when he first started making contributions. Since then, he has lost contact with that representative and has not received any ongoing advice from any representative of the vendor. He would like to know if his allocations are suitable.

Solution: George should determine if there is a guaranteed death benefit associated with his annuity contract and carefully consider whether that is a benefit that he would like to continue. If not, he is allowed to transact a nontaxable transfer of his assets from his annuity contract to an account with a mutual fund vendor in his university's plan. This will allow George to avoid the extra expense associated with his annuity contract so that he is paying only the management expenses associated with the mutual funds in which he invests.

Case Study 5: Take Advantage of After-Tax Savings

Scenario: Larry is three years from retirement and is currently contributing the maximum allowable to his 403(b) account. He and his wife both work and have no debt; as a result, their net income far exceeds their day-to-day needs. Unfortunately, their combined incomes place them in a 40 percent federal and state tax bracket. Larry and his wife estimate that they have $1,500 of after-tax money available beyond their needs each month. They would like to reduce their taxes.

Solution: Because Larry is within three years of retirement, he can use the general catch-up that allows him to contribute $33,000 to a 457(b) account. Since contributions to his 457(b) are made on a before-tax basis, he will be able to contribute $2,500 per month with a resulting decrease of $1,500 per month in his net take-home pay from the university. Larry and his wife achieve their goal of reducing their taxes by $12,000 per year and have not negatively affected their lifestyle.

Chapter 3

Limitations of University Retirement Plans

It Is Important to Have Options

Well managed, robust portfolios provide a high degree of flexibility and control over the investment options available to the investor. Having the ability to choose among a broad choice of investments allows an investor to potentially achieve a higher return, moderate risk more effectively, and better manage liquidity needs in retirement. The choices available to academics in their university-sponsored retirement plans are dictated by IRS and employer constraints, the diversity of account types owned by the investor, and triggering events that can be taken advantage of in order to take control of certain retirement plan assets.

The Desired Spectrum of Equity-Based Investments

Ideally, an investor should have access to equity investments that include individual stocks, **diversified mutual funds** (including **open-end mutual funds** and **closed-end mutual funds**), **sector mutual funds,** and ETFs.

Diversified mutual fund: An investment vehicle designed to reduce exposure to risk by diversifying among many publicly traded companies and several industries.

Open-end mutual fund: A fund operated by an investment company that invests in one or more categories of assets, including stocks, bonds, and money market instruments. Investors can redeem mutual fund shares on demand. Mutual funds offer investors diversification and professional money management. A management fee is charged for these services, and there may be other expenses. Funds with a sales charge are called load funds, while those sold without commission are called no-load funds.

Closed-end mutual fund: A fund company that issues and trades shares like any other corporation and usually does not redeem its shares. These funds are a collection of stocks and/or bonds and may trade at a premium or a discount to its intrinsic value.

Sector mutual fund: A mutual fund that concentrates on a relatively narrow market sector (such as utilities or technology companies). These funds can experience higher price volatility than a diversified fund.

Many of these options allow strategic targeting of investments into sectors that might provide a balance between risk and return consistent with prevailing financial markets, economic conditions, and an individual's risk tolerance. Exchange traded funds in particular allow investors to invest in targeted sectors with funds that impose relatively low expense ratios. Other opportunities, such as closed-end mutual funds, could present opportunities for accessing certain investment types at discounts to current market valuations of the underlying securities.

Equity-based mutual funds are defined by the fund's **investment style** and the size or **capitalization** of the companies held in the fund. The combination of style and capitalization establishes the asset class of a fund. Figure 1 shows an asset allocation matrix used to describe **asset classes** for mutual funds. This matrix applies to both domestic and foreign equity mutual funds.

Investment style: Established by the types of stock; value, or growth held in a fund.

Capitalization: The total market value of a company, calculated by multiplying the company's outstanding shares by the current share price.

Asset class: The combination of market capitalization and investment style.

Figure 1 - Characterizing Equity Mutual Funds by Asset Class*

Style

		Value	Blend	Growth
	Large	LV	LB	LG
Market Cap	Mid	MV	MB	MG
	Small	SV	SB	SG

* LV = Large Cap Value; LB = Large Cap Blend; LG = Large Cap Growth;
MV = Mid Cap Value; MB = Mid Cap Blend; MG = Mid Cap Growth;
SV = Small Cap Value; SB = Small Cap Blend; SG = Small Cap Growth

Value funds generally contain mature companies that in many cases pay dividends. **Growth funds** contain firms that are less mature. Rather than paying dividends to stock owners, these companies are often more likely to invest in research or new product development. For example, Duke Energy is generally considered a value stock, while Intel is typically thought of as a growth stock. A blended fund, sometimes called a core fund, contains both growth and value stocks.

> <u>Value fund</u>: A mutual fund that favors buying stocks with lower price-to-earnings ratios and relatively high dividend yields, such as cyclical companies and companies found in mature industries.
>
> <u>Growth funds</u>: Investment vehicles designed to provide shareholders with growth of capital by investing in companies with a history of rapidly growing earnings and generally higher price-to-earnings ratios. Growth funds are generally more volatile than value funds, rising faster in bull markets and dropping more sharply in bear markets.

The median market capitalization of the stocks in a fund defines the size dimension in the asset allocation matrix. The following are the generally accepted demarcations for delineating between capitalization levels:

➢ Large Cap – Companies with capitalizations of greater than $10 billion
➢ Mid Cap – Companies with market capitalizations of between $2 and $10 billion
➢ Small Cap – Companies with market capitalization of between $300 million and $2 billion.

In practice, many diversified funds invest most of their assets in one asset class but may have significant proportions in other asset classes, as shown in Figure 2. This is commonly true for large funds that may have difficulty finding a sufficient number of quality investments within a single asset class. In fact, this is one of the primary reasons for funds to be closed to new investors, i.e., accepting additional cash inflows might require a change in investment objective or holding an excessive cash position.

Figure 2 - Most Mutual Funds Consist of Multiple Asset Classes

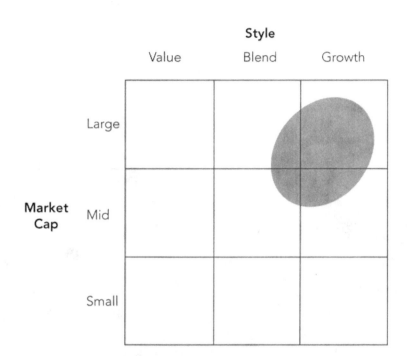

A single asset class, style, or capitalization will not consistently provide the highest or lowest returns. The performance of different asset classes depends upon the current stage of the economic cycle, the overall volatility of the market, market interest rates, and consumer and government spending, along with a number of other factors. The relative performance of each asset group shown in Figure 1 and Figure 2 changes over time, and the absolute performance of any asset group is loosely correlated to that of other asset groups. These characteristics are the basis for the asset allocation approach to asset management.

The relative performance of the six basic asset groups for the period 1999–2008 is shown in Figure 3. The asset group with the best performance for any year is shown at the top of each column followed by those with decreasingly lower returns. Significant changes in performance can be detected over smaller time frames. However for diversified funds, reacting to these movements over short time frames might not be in the investor's best interest. It is important, however, to follow the relative performance of these different asset groups and to modify the weighting of each in a portfolio to reflect relative valuations as well as anticipated relative performance based upon the current phase of the economic cycle and other financial and economic factors.

Figure 3 - Returns By Asset Class

1999	2000	2001	2002	2003	2004	2005	2006	2007	2008
52.46 MG	24.59 MV	18.58 SV	-8.24 SV	52.65 SG	24.30 MV	16.27 MG	25.79 LV	19.70 MG	-31.67 SV
46.80 SG	18.65 SV	5.06 MV	-10.00 MV	48.87 SV	24.03 SV	11.54 MV	20.03 SV	12.34 LG	-35.95 MV
42.59 LG	5.66 LV	-3.38 LV	-15.05 LV	40.02 MG	15.45 MG	7.04 LV	18.81 MV	11.08 SG	-36.11 LV
0.57 LV	-11.10 MG	-12.92 SG	-32.54 MG	35.93 MV	14.05 LV	5.77 SG	10.04 SG	-0.43 LV	-39.92 SG
-5.19 SV	-12.10 SG	-21.59 MG	-33.15 LG	30.65 LG	13.48 SG	5.12 SV	9.63 MG	-5.52 MV	-41.87 LG
-6.83 MV	-33.51 LG	-29.07 LG	-36.87 SG	26.26 LV	0.19 LG	3.43 LG	5.68 LG	-8.15 SV	-46.28 MG

Source: Compiled from information at Morningstar.com

The Desired Spectrum of Fixed-Income Options

Similarly, an investor would want to have access to a variety of fixed-income investments. Fixed annuities, **stable value accounts of annuities**, bond mutual funds, individual corporate and government bonds, FDIC-insured certificates of deposit, and **money market mutual funds** all play a part in a well-designed fixed-income portfolio.

> **Stable value accounts of annuities:** Accounts that seek to preserve principal and pay current interest rates. These are similar to fixed annuities. They usually offer few if any guarantees but also have fewer withdrawal restrictions.
>
> **Money market mutual funds:** Funds that hold short-term debt securities, such as commercial paper, certificates of deposit, and treasury bills, with a maturity of one year or less. Typically, these are safe, highly liquid investments.

Fixed-income investments are characterized by the interest rate or **yield**, their **maturity**, **credit quality,** and the investment's **liquidity**. An individual investor must have the freedom to move between fixed-income options with differing defining characteristics in order to efficiently manage this critical portfolio component.

> **Yield:** The annual income return on an investment, expressed as a percentage of the price. For stocks, yield is the annual dividend divided by the current price, also known as a dividend yield. For bonds, it is the coupon rate divided by the market price, called current yield. For example, a bond selling for $1,000 with a 10 percent coupon ($100 coupon payment) offers a 10 percent current yield. If that bond's price rises to $1,500, the yield would fall to 6.7 percent for individuals that purchase at that higher price.
>
> **Maturity:** The date when a debt becomes due for payment. A bond due to mature on June 1, 2015, will return the bondholder's principal and final interest payment on that date.
>
> **Credit quality:** A measure of a bond issuer's ability to pay interest and principal in a timely manner.
>
> **Liquidity:** The ability to buy or sell an asset quickly without substantially affecting the asset's price.

Bond mutual funds may consist of hundreds of different bond issues with varying maturities, yields, and quality. Bond mutual funds can be classified by the predominating time to maturity and credit quality of the bonds in the fund as shown in Figure 4. Prevailing interest rates, the credit environment, and current rates of inflation will dictate the types of individual bonds or bond funds that might present the most value to an investor. One must keep in mind that the market value of bonds, and therefore of bond funds, does fluctuate over time and is especially sensitive to changes in market interest rates. As market interest rates rise, bond values will generally decline. The market value of bonds with longer maturities and lower credit quality will be impacted most by these interest rate changes.

Figure 4 – Characterizing Bond Mutual Funds by Maturity and Credit Quality

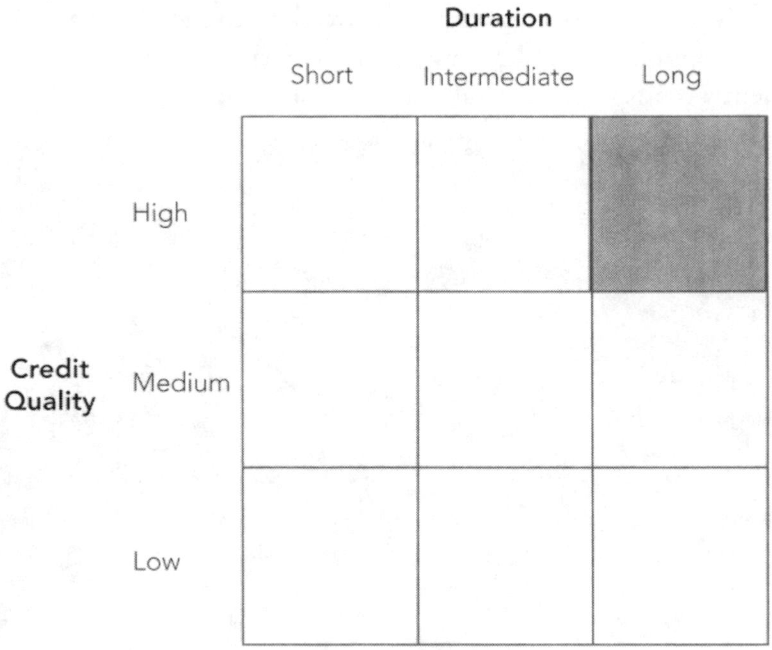

Duration

	Short	Intermediate	Long
High			▓▓▓
Medium			
Low			

Credit Quality

Variable annuities do pose some negatives as we discussed in Chapter 2; however, there is a place for fixed annuities and stable value funds in your portfolio based upon your liquidity needs and the degree to which these instruments' yield or rate of return is competitive with other alternatives.

Access to a full menu of fixed-income options allows a portfolio to be constructed and managed to achieve a proper balance between risk, liquidity, and return. This is of prime importance during retirement, when the investor must receive income from his portfolio. Having the flexibility to access a wide variety of fixed-income investments to efficiently receive income during retirement is a critical component of retirement planning that we'll discuss in more detail later.

University Retirement Plans May Limit Your Choices

To reiterate, the IRS, your university employer, and university vendors impose investment constraints on university retirement accounts. The IRS dictates the investment types available to investors, and the university further limits the particular investment options by its selection of vendors. Vendors, in conjunction with the university, in turn can limit your access to a set of investment options within their products.

The IRS creates the first level of control by constraining investors to mutual funds and annuity products in certain plan types. Because the university, or in some cases the state, bears fiduciary responsibility for these plans, the investment options are often limited to a relatively small number of specific diversified mutual funds and/or annuity options with each vendor.

Also, most vendors impose restrictions on the amount and timing of withdrawals from fixed annuities and stable value accounts. This can dramatically constrain the liquid assets available for retirement income. Many academics are not aware that the primary provider of mandatory university retirement plans restricts access to certain fixed-income accounts by imposing a nine-year payout of these assets. This vendor is not unique in imposing such constraints. Recognizing these obstacles and taking action in a timely manner to alleviate this impact on liquidity is critical as one's retirement years approach.

Biases of Vendors Within University-Sponsored Retirement Plans

Representatives of university retirement plan vendors receive pay from their employer and therefore have an inherent conflict. As employees of a vendor, their responsibility is to place assets in that vendor's product. It is unlikely that a single vendor, with limited investment choices, can provide for an optimum portfolio design that incorporates a breadth of fixed-income and variable investments.

The representative of a university vendor is probably not going to tell you that you need to invest some of your assets with a competitor. However, for those with large balances in a restrictive university plan, that is exactly the approach that needs to be followed. Nor is it likely that such a representative will be inclined to share with you that certain aspects of another vendor's product may be more suitable for your particular needs, or that a competitor may offer investments that have a history of better performance than those offered in their product. Again, it is all about creating the opportunity for you to have choices. Also ask yourself these questions:

> ➤ During the course of your employment, how many times have you personally met with a representative of your vendor?
> ➤ How many different representatives of that vendor have you had telephone conversations with?
> ➤ Do you have accounts that the vendor is not aware of and has therefore never asked how those assets are allocated in order to avoid redundancy?
> ➤ When was the last time a representative of that vendor proactively approached you to suggest that you make changes in your account?
> ➤ After your employer makes you aware of subtle plan changes such as the addition or deletion of mutual funds from the plan, are you called by the representative to explain what these changes may mean to you?

Many investors also do not understand the manner in which interest rates on fixed-income investments are calculated and credited to accounts by some vendors. In times of rising interest rates, vendors may continue to credit your account with rates that were in effect when your money was contributed, or if you made a change in allocation, when your money was reinvested. Some vendors allow internal transfers within their product that make the "contribution date" current, resulting in an increase in the interest rate paid. If you are not aware of these protocols, you will not be taking full advantage of the opportunities available to you to achieve a higher rate of return on some of your fixed-income investments.

If you step back from this self-perpetuating approach and take a more complete and comprehensive attitude, whether you do this alone or with an independent advisor's help, you may find at the end of the day that your portfolio might stand on a firmer foundation.

Case Studies

Case Study 1: You Should Be Aware of Ongoing Changes to Your Retirement Plans

Scenario: Martha has only had one faculty position, which she has held for 25 years. Her only retirement account is her mandatory defined contribution retirement plan. She opened her account when she was hired, with little evaluation of her alternatives. She has not significantly changed her allocation during that entire period. She is aware that her employer has added additional vendors to the plan, but she has never been approached by a representative of any of the new vendors, nor is the vendor that she currently invests with proactive in contacting her to ask if she would like to meet to review her allocation. Her interactions with her current vendor have been limited to brief telephone conversations with whoever happens to answer the phone when she calls.

Solution: Martha's investment options need to be reevaluated. She determines that she has invested her assets into three mutual funds — all of them large cap funds with one vendor — and that the fixed-income account with that vendor pays the lowest rate of return of any of the options available in her plan. Martha decides to split her assets between two vendors, to reallocate some of her assets into mid cap and small cap funds, and to begin investing in a foreign stock mutual fund. She also begins the process of dividing the assets in her fixed-income account between her current vendor and another vendor that is paying a slightly higher rate of return and has less onerous restrictions on withdrawals.

Case Study 2: Understand the Withdrawal Restrictions on Your Fixed-Income Investments

Scenario: George is 61 and wants to retire when he reaches age 65. He knows he will need access to his fixed-income assets but has just found out that he must take those out over a nine-year period. The stock market is down considerably, and he believes it will take at least five years for the market to recover. George doesn't want to sell investments in the stock market before it has time to recover.

Solution: George should begin the "payout" of fixed-income assets immediately so that approximately one half will be available to him when he retires. George completes the paperwork to begin the annual payment of these assets and chooses to have them invested in two bond funds available within his vendor's plan.

Case Study 3: Periodically Evaluate the Investments Offered by Vendors in Your Retirement Plans

Scenario: Abigail has a mandatory retirement plan and a supplemental 403(b) with her current university employer. Because she hasn't taken the time to investigate all her options, she has chosen, for convenience, to place both of these accounts with a single, large university vendor. Fortunately, she has distributed her investments across various asset classes. She is now wondering if she's missing an opportunity to invest in mutual funds with a history of better performance that are available with other vendors.

Solution: Abigail should investigate the funds offered by the other vendors in her plan and, if appropriate, restructure her portfolio by placing some of her assets with one of the other vendors in her university plans. This will give her the ability to invest in a wider spectrum of funds and will provide her with more flexibility to increase her portfolio's overall return in the future.

Case Study 4: Don't Assume That Bond Mutual Funds Can't Lose Value

Scenario: John has a bond mutual fund in his mandatory retirement plan and uses the interest he earns to partially furnish his retirement income. The fund primarily holds bonds with long maturities --- most maturing in more than 15 years. John reads an article that suggests that the country may be entering a period of sharp increases in inflation that could erode the purchasing power of the interest he receives on his bond fund.

Solution: John investigates his options and finds an inflation-protected bond fund in his plan that he didn't know existed. The fund ensures that the yield on his bonds will increase along with the rate of inflation. He invests half of his holding in this fund to help protect him from a significant decrease in purchasing power in future years. Because he has also read that this increase in inflation may drive interest rates higher and the market value of his bond fund lower, he decides to invest the other half of the assets in his current bond fund into a money market mutual fund.

Chapter 4

Opportunities Presented by University Retirement Plans

Many university faculty and staff are surprised to learn of the opportunities they have to make wider use of their investment options and the flexibility they have to remove assets from confining university retirement accounts. Efficiently restructuring your portfolio begins by starting with the most restrictive plan and making best use of the options it provides. This should be followed by sequentially addressing less constraining accounts. For the many reasons mentioned in previous chapters, when possible, you should consider taking advantage of **rollover** and **transfer** opportunities to expand the investment options available to you.

Rollover: A tax-free reinvestment of a distribution from a retirement plan into an IRA or other qualified plan, providing the reinvestment is completed within 60 days of the distribution.

Transfer: Moving funds from one account to another of the same type. For example, the act of moving funds from one IRA to another IRA or from one 403(b) to a second 403(b).

Before completing a rollover or transfer, you should be careful to identify and evaluate any aspects of the plan that might be advantageous to you. For example, some supplemental retirement plans have loan provisions that are not available in an IRA. Also, if you have assets in a variable annuity, there may be surrender charges associated with relinquishing your contract. Further, some annuity contracts contain unique provisions that you may want to preserve. As you evaluate alternative actions with respect to variable annuities, you should also consider any contract expenses imposed and the limited number of investment opportunities inherent in these contracts.

Figure 5 illustrates the fundamental issues involved in managing an academic's portfolio. This hierarchal approach is first driven by the constraints of a mandatory retirement plan (mandatory plans owned by spouses should be considered at this stage), followed by those inherent in the usually less restrictive, but still constraining, supplemental plans. The process should then expand to include accounts not governed by university constraints. This latter set of accounts might include other assets unaffiliated with an employer as well as accounts created from a university plan as a result of a triggering event such as termination of employment from a previous university employer. These accounts, such as IRAs and nonretirement accounts provide an opportunity for accessing investments that complement those selected in more restrictive accounts to produce a well-balanced portfolio.

Figure 5 - Expanding Your Universe of Investment Choices

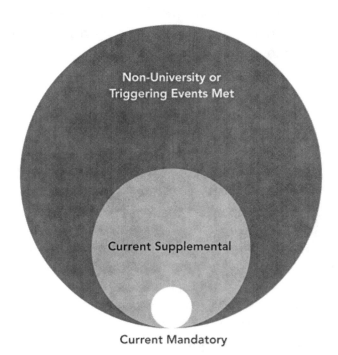

To reiterate, the goal of this process is to formulate a plan that incorporates all accounts into a cohesive portfolio and takes advantage of the benefits of diversification across asset classes for equity investments and a high degree of control over fixed-income investments. These various accounts should communicate with each other so that the end result is an efficient, well-balanced set of accounts that achieve your specific goals by taking advantage of the strengths and flexibility offered by each.

Flexibility of Mandatory University-Sponsored Retirement Plans

If an investor has selected a defined benefit plan as a mandatory option, then no more decisions regarding this plan can be made until a retirement income option is selected. As long as the employer offering this plan is financially sound, the investor should consider these assets as a fixed-income account when making decisions regarding the other aspects of his or her portfolio.

In most cases, university-sponsored mandatory defined contribution plans are more restrictive and offer fewer investment choices than supplemental plans. There may be only one vendor in the mandatory plan, and even those plans with multiple vendors often restrict the investment options to one fund in each asset class per vendor. In some cases, plans do not offer mutual funds within all asset classes. Also, as mentioned previously, it is not unusual for a fund to be so large that it does not have a distinct asset class.

Given these factors, the mandatory plan is the place to begin when constructing an efficient portfolio. However, it is incumbent upon the investor to conduct his or her due diligence to the extent that a clear picture is available of the investment choices in this plan.

For mutual funds, one should at minimum have an understanding of a fund's historical performance compared to other funds in the same asset class and the tenure of the current fund managers. It is also helpful to have some sense of the major holdings in the fund, particularly the largest sector holdings. We have just experienced a time when funds that held a large percentage of financial stocks suffered some of the largest losses. One should also investigate each fund to ensure that its advertised investment objective is a true reflection of the manner in which the assets in the fund are invested. As mentioned in the previous chapter, a fund that is advertised as a large cap growth fund does not ensure that the fund is managed entirely to that objective or that its performance will track that of funds in that asset class.

For fixed-income investments, the investor should be aware of the current rate of return, the length of time (if any) over which this return is guaranteed, and the restrictions that are imposed upon withdrawals from the fixed account. These parameters should be matched to the individual's liquidity requirements and the availability of better alternatives offered by other vendors and those available in other accounts.

For plans that offer multiple vendors, it would be highly unlikely for a single vendor to offer the best fund in every asset class. Figure 6 depicts a hypothetical scenario in which a mandatory plan includes four vendors and shows, for each asset class, the vendor with the best performing fund over a specified period of time. This figure shows a situation in which multiple providers demonstrate strengths in distinct asset classes.

Figure 6 - Multiple Vendors Are Often Advantageous

		Style	
	Value	Blend	Growth
Large	Vendor 1	Vendor 3	Vendor 3
Mid	Vendor 4	Vendor 2	Vendor 1
Small	Vendor 2	Vendor 4	Vendor 1

(Row labels under **Market Cap**: Large, Mid, Small)

The investor should identify the best options within this plan regardless of vendor. Often — and especially for people with large balances in their mandatory plan — it may be in the investor's best interest to have multiple vendors.

Strengths can change over time; thus, this type of analysis should be conducted periodically, which further suggests the need for an engaged approach to managing your portfolio. The variability of relative performance between funds within the same asset class is precisely the reason that multiple providers could be beneficial. You would want multiple vendors even if the relative ranking of funds was static, so long as no one vendor had the "best" fund in each asset class, which is improbable. By following this approach, the investor has the flexibility to liquidate a fund held by one vendor that may have performed well in the past but is now showing a pattern of underperformance, and to purchase a better fund within that asset class in a second vendor's product.

Diversified mutual funds that meet an investor's asset allocation requirement are available in mandatory plans, and the investor's goal should be to have access to as many of these funds as possible. Creating choices is the gateway to flexibility. Don't be afraid of having multiple mandatory plan vendors. In some cases, such as when mandatory plan assets are a smaller percentage of total assets, an investor could reasonably maintain assets with only one provider. However, the investor should concentrate her holdings in the one, two, or three best funds available in her mandatory plan and then use the remaining assets in her portfolio to invest in other asset classes in other accounts to satisfy her asset allocation requirements.

Complementing Mandatory Plans With Participation in Supplemental Plans

Supplemental plans often provide investment options that can be used to complement those available in mandatory plans. Effective management of assets in these plans can frequently enhance the risk/return profile of both the equity and fixed-income portions of an investor's portfolio.

In some cases, vendors in various supplemental plans are the same as those in the mandatory plan, with significant overlap of investment offerings across plans. In other cases, vendors may be distinctly different, or the same vendor may have different offerings in the two plans. After selecting the best funds in the mandatory plan, the investor should identify funds in various supplemental plans that strengthen the portfolio by investment in those asset classes that are missing or have been under-allocated in the mandatory plan.

Using Triggering Events to Add Flexibility and Efficiency

Table 2 and Table 3 identify investment options that are both allowed by the IRS and are generally made available in university-sponsored plans. This is in contrasdt to the broad availability of various investment options in brokerage IRA and after-tax accounts. The constraints described previously can limit an investor's choices and therefore constrain the investor's opportunity to improve efficiency, flexibility, and strategic focus in his or her portfolio. Although IRS regulations now allow ETFs in some university-sponsored plans, they are not commonly allowed by universities. In addition to the limitations on equity-based investments, the constraints can restrict fixed-income investments, blocking the investor from decreasing her risk and enhancing the liquidity of her assets.

Table 2 – Commonly Allowable Equity Investment Options

Account Type	Individual Stocks	Open-Ended Div. Mutual Funds	Closed End Mutual Funds	Sector Mutual Funds	Exchange Traded Funds	Variable Annuities
Mandatory Retirement Plan		✓				✓
403(b)		✓				✓
457(b)		✓				✓
401(k)		✓				✓
IRA	✓	✓	✓	✓	✓	✓
After Tax	✓	✓	✓	✓	✓	✓

Table 3 – Allowable Fixed-Income Investment Options

Account Type	Fixed Annuities	Stable Value Accounts of Annuities	Bond Mutual Funds	Individual Corp. & Gov. Bonds	FDIC-Insured Certificates of Deposit	Money Market Mutual Funds
Mandatory Retirement Plan	✓	✓	✓			✓
403(b)	✓	✓	✓			✓
457(b)	✓	✓	✓			✓
401(k)	✓	✓	✓			✓
IRA	✓	✓	✓	✓	✓	✓
After Tax	✓	✓	✓	✓	✓	✓

University employers have the authority to further limit allowable investment options beyond those imposed by the IRS. For example, it is uncommon for mandatory plans to allow sector mutual funds.

Two triggering events are critical to the investor: termination of employment or attaining age 59 ½. These events are conditions that often allow the investor to rollover certain assets from university retirement accounts to IRAs that convey control to the investor.

Termination of employment generally allows an individual to rollover assets in that employer's retirement plans into an IRA. In most cases, rollovers can be completed from both mandatory and supplemental plans. A small number of universities, primarily private universities, prohibit rollovers of mandatory plan assets or constrain rollovers until a certain age is attained. Also, the investor should be careful to consider other factors that may be unique to her employer's plan that, if ignored, could be a detriment to the investor.

For example, those hired at any University of North Carolina campus on or before August 12, 1989, do not have to pay North Carolina state income tax on their ORP assets when they are withdrawn as long as these assets are distributed from an ORP account. Rolling these assets into an IRA subjects them to state income tax upon withdrawal. This is yet another reason for the investor to make the best use of all the vendor options in a plan with this type of limitation. Also, in North Carolina, upon retirement, participants must receive a monthly lifetime income from their ORP assets in order to continue receiving health insurance benefits.

This same tax treatment also applies to 401(k) and 457(b) (deferred compensation plan) assets accumulated while employed at UNC system campuses. For these accounts, two conditions must be met to avoid state income tax: 1) contributions must have begun prior to August 12, 1989; and 2) the assets must remain in one of these accounts until taxable distributions are taken.

Recent federal legislation further limits the transportability of supplemental 403(b) assets accumulated with a university employer while still employed by that university. Before these rule changes, a participant was free to perform a nontaxable transfer of these assets to any 403(b) vendor of her choice. Although these specific transactions are no longer allowed, a participant can still transfer assets between vendors within a university plan.

Finally, reaching the age of 59 ½ provides the investor with the opportunity to rollover certain university retirement plan assets. Some private universities allow the employee, even while employed, to rollover employee contributions and associated earnings from mandatory plans once this age is attained. Also, supplemental 401(k) and 403(b) assets can generally be rolled over to an IRA at 59 ½ even though the investor may still be employed by the university at which the assets were accumulated.

This triggering age does not allow the rollover of 457(b) assets with an investor's current employer. Deferred compensation or 457(b) accounts operate under two significantly different rules from other university-sponsored plans. First, attainment of age 59 ½ is not a triggering event that allows a rollover. Second, once an investor has terminated employment, the assets accumulated while at that employer can be withdrawn without incurring the normal 10 percent early withdrawal penalty imposed by the IRS, regardless of age. There is also an IRS rule regarding distributions from 401(k) and 403(b) accounts that most university academics are not aware of. This rule allows investors to receive distributions from 401(k) and 403(b) accounts and avoid the 10% early withdrawal penalty if they have separated from service and attained the age of 55 before separating from service. This suggests that a 457(b) account might be considered a supplemental account of first choice by those that anticipate separating from service with their current employer before age 55.

Using Non-University Accounts to Complete the Puzzle

Many university employees have assets that were never affiliated with university service. These may include traditional IRAs, Roth IRAs, nonretirement accounts, and accounts owned by spouses. IRAs and after-tax nonretirement accounts offer the greatest range of investment options. Spousal employer-sponsored accounts will have their own unique characteristics with respect to rollovers and transfers.

After-tax accounts can provide an opportunity to take advantage of current special tax treatment on gains, losses, and dividend payments. Current rules allow long-term capital gains and qualified dividends to be taxed at either a 5 percent or 15 percent federal tax rate depending upon an individual's ordinary income tax rate.

These accounts also offer a degree of flexibility during the retirement income phase. Since the principal in these accounts has previously been taxed, withdrawals from these accounts during retirement can be used to manage taxable income efficiently.

For instance, distributions from retirement accounts could be delayed, and instead, income could be taken entirely from after-tax accounts until those accounts have been depleted. In the extreme, this could result in reducing taxable income to zero. This would allow retirement assets to continue to grow tax-deferred. Alternatively, withdrawals from after-tax accounts could be made in tandem with distributions from retirement accounts in order to reduce the marginal tax rate to a nonzero value over a longer period of time.

Case Studies

Case Study 1: Previous Employer Accounts Can Help You Expand Your Equity-Based Investment Options

Scenario: Franklin is 54, has been with his current employer for 10 years, and has been funding an ORP account as well as a supplemental 403(b) account at a moderate level for the past eight years. He has 18 years of previous employment with another university where he had an ORP account as his mandatory plan and a supplemental 403(b) account. All four of these accounts are with the same vendor. After realizing that his retirement accounts have been somewhat ignored over the years, Franklin realizes now that it would be to his advantage to expand his equity-based investments to include other mutual funds.

Solution: Since there is a high degree of overlap of funds available in his four university-sponsored plans, Franklin decides to rollover both of the retirement accounts with his previous employer into a single IRA. For now, he would like to invest most of the IRA assets into diversified mutual funds and has determined that the foreign funds available in his current employer's plan are its weakest component. Franklin reallocates his assets to sell the foreign funds in his current employer's plan and purchase better foreign funds in his IRA.

Case Study 2: Previous Employer Accounts Can Help You Expand Your Fixed-Income Investment Options

Scenario: Eleanor is 58 and is starting to seriously plan for her retirement, which she hopes to begin in seven years. She has retirement accounts from a previous university employer in addition to a mandatory plan with her current employer. She is concerned that all of her "safe" fixed-income assets are invested with a single vendor that imposes significant restrictions on withdrawals. Also, since this vendor is an insurance company, Eleanor's assets are not backed by FDIC insurance, so she has two valid reasons to look for other options.

Solution: Eleanor rolls her previous employer plans into an IRA and begins to purchase a mix of CDs and high-quality corporate bonds. These have varying maturities, which help her better manage access to her fixed-income assets. They also provide her the flexibility to invest in higher interest instruments should interest rates increase. Further, Eleanor decides to begin taking assets from the fixed-income investments in her current mandatory plan by transferring these assets in 10 essentially equal payments, as required by her current vendor, into two bond mutual funds with this vendor.

Case Study 3: Attaining Age 59 ½ Triggers Your Ability to Rollover Supplemental Plan Assets

Scenario: James is 60 and has been with his current employer for his entire career. He chose the state's defined benefit plan as his mandatory plan. Additionally, he has been contributing the maximum to his 401(k) for most of his career and has seen the account grow to a relatively large balance. Unfortunately, the plan provides him very few investment options. James wants access to a larger number of investment options with his 401(k) assets.

Solution: James could rollover his 401(k) assets into an IRA where he can begin to invest in a wider variety of mutual funds. This will also lay the groundwork for his investing some of his assets into sector mutual funds and a wider assortment of social awareness funds — a philosophical approach that he wants to pursue. Before completing this rollover, he should ensure that the rollover will not have any adverse tax consequences.

Case Study 4: Make Sure You Understand the Restrictions Placed on Your Fixed-Income Accounts

Scenario: Dolley will retire next year. The only retirement assets she has are in her mandatory plan. She has determined that she will need to withdraw $70,000 per year from her accounts once she retires. Knowing that she needs to keep five years of retirement income out of stock market investments, she realizes that she needs to invest approximately $350,000 into fixed-income investments. She is trying to determine how to best invest this $350,000 and believes that it should be allocated into the fixed account of her current vendor. She is not aware that this vendor restricts withdrawals to approximately 10 percent of the principal plus earnings per year. Based upon these withdrawal parameters, she will receive approximately $42,000 per year once she begins her withdrawals.

Solution: Dolley will be making a mistake if she follows through on her plans. If her retirement coincides with a long-term bear market, she will have to sell equity assets that are down in value since she will only receive about 60 percent of her required annual income from her fixed-income income investments when she retires. Dolley should reposition her assets so that her fixed-income assets are split between bond funds and a money market fund.

Case Study 5: You Can Access Individual Stocks and Other Targeted Investments With Previous Employer Account Assets

Scenario: Harry is 45 years old and has retirement plans with two previous university employers. He wants to invest in individual stocks, sector funds, and diversified mutual funds not available in his current employer plan.

Solution: Harry can rollover the assets in the retirement plans of his previous employers into a single IRA. This allows him to invest these assets and better target his investing while complementing the relatively constrained investments of his current employer's plan.

Case Study 6: Gaining Access to a Larger Number of Socially Conscious Mutual Funds

Scenario: Bess has retirement plans from two previous university employers and has a strong interest in social investing. She has a particular interest in investing assets into "green" funds that invest in companies that are manufacturing wind and solar energy systems. Her current university-sponsored plan only offers one social awareness fund

Solution: As with Harry, Bess can rollover the assets in her previous employers' plans to an IRA. This rollover transaction gives her access to a wide variety of funds that are compatible with her investment objectives and not otherwise available in her current employer's plan.

Chapter 5

Guidelines for Retirement Planning

The Cookie-Cutter Approach to Investment Management

There has been a recent trend toward offering so-called **target retirement date mutual funds** as investment vehicles. These funds generally have as their constituents a number of diversified equity and fixed-income mutual funds. For this reason, they fit into a broader classification referred to as a "fund of funds."

> **Target retirement date mutual funds:** Mutual funds with an asset allocation mix among stocks, bonds, and short-term instruments that are more aggressive for younger investors and become more conservative as investors approach retirement.

Target retirement date funds are designed to shift to a larger fixed-income allocation as an individual becomes older. By establishing your retirement year, the funds attempt to modify the allocation inside the fund to an appropriate risk level for your age. The allocation between equity and bond funds may vary widely for the same target-date from one vendor to another. This lack of consistency makes it difficult for an investor to rely upon the target-date as a determinant of the allocation within the fund. Many plan vendors will now automatically enroll an investor into a target retirement date fund if no instructions have been provided as to the specific fund(s) into which monthly contributions should be invested.

These funds also fail to allow for the many factors that should influence the management of an individual's portfolio. For example, they do not allow for the kind of portfolio management that can take advantage of the dynamics of equity and fixed-income asset classes or an investor's unique financial circumstances and preferences.

The Investment Life Cycle

As mentioned earlier, the performance of various equity asset classes is loosely correlated. That is, these asset classes perform differently with respect to each other over time. This variability allows one to take profits and to purchase asset classes at favorable prices. Target-date funds do not allow the individual investor to take advantage of these market dynamics. Few would suggest that selling indiscriminately across all assets in your portfolio is the best strategy for producing income in retirement. But that is exactly what happens when an investor sells shares of a target-date fund in order to receive retirement income. This same inefficiency occurs when an investor makes additional purchases with his monthly contributions. All asset groups in the target-date fund are purchased regardless of their recent performance or prospective future returns.

A superior approach to retirement planning is to instead establish and manage assets consistent with a retirement planning life cycle that consists of three distinct phases as shown in Figure 7. This approach divides this life cycle into phases that are characterized by the distinct investment approach required during each.

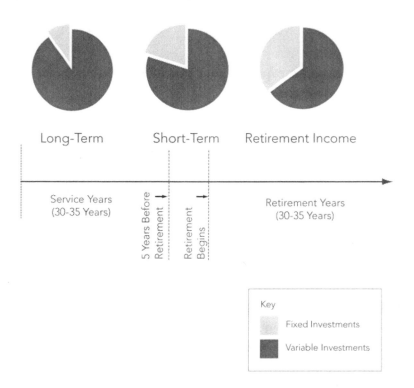

Figure 7 - The Investment Life Cycle

An investor would normally have an increasing allocation to fixed-income investments as they progress through the investment life cycle. This is not inconsistent with the global approach taken by target retirement date funds. The difference in the two methods lies in the fact that any single target retirement date fund treats each investor the same and does not allow for tactical targeting of purchase and sell decisions.

The first two phases shown in Figure 7, long-term accumulation and short-term accumulation, encompass those years in which the investor is employed and is accumulating retirement assets due to the contributions that are being made to the portfolio and the growth of these assets. The final phase encompasses the retirement years during which an investor would ideally have the largest portion of his portfolio set aside into fixed-income investments, both to preserve wealth, and to efficiently manage the withdrawals needed to fund retirement income. The exact allocation between equity and fixed-income investments within each of these phases will depend upon many factors including:

➤ Personal preferences
➤ Aversion to risk
➤ The need for exposing your portfolio to risk in order to meet retirement goals
➤ The relative performance of fixed and equity-based investments
➤ The level of retirement income needed

These factors along with others such as the rate of savings and the actual equity and fixed-income returns over time work together to establish the growth and depletion of assets through the investment life cycle. We have developed analysis tools that track the growth of assets during these accumulation phases and accounts for the withdrawal of assets from the portfolio during the retirement income phase. We attempt to map a band of uncertainty associated with the possible change in portfolio value as depicted in Figure 8. This is accomplished by assuming various scenarios of retirement date, return on assets, fixed-income allocation for each phase, contribution rates, etc. Obviously there can be widely differing results depending upon the values assigned to these parameters.

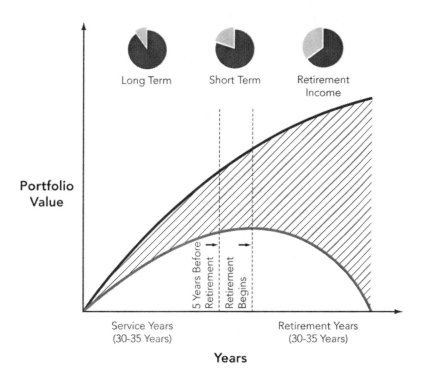

Figure 8 - Range of Retirement Outcomes

This approach helps investors:

➤ Determine if their investments are on target to reach retirement goals
➤ Establish the level of investment risk they need to meet their goals
➤ Ascertain necessary adjustments in savings patterns
➤ Examine the tradeoffs between desired retirement income and retirement age

The uncertainty inherent in the retirement planning process requires that ongoing reassessments be conducted to determine if intermediate targets along the investment life cycle are being met.

Long-Term Accumulation Phase

The long-term accumulation phase spans from initial employment until approximately five years from retirement. This phase is often characterized by the highest level of portfolio risk and therefore an asset allocation that is significantly weighted toward equities. Exposure to higher levels of risk 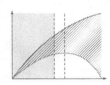 and therefore the potential for higher returns in this phase is consistent with the length of the investment time horizon that gives the investor a significant period of time to recover from market downturns and therefore the capability to accept the associated risk.

The growth of your portfolio during this phase is the primary determinant that will dictate to a large degree whether you will meet your retirement goals. The growth, and ultimately the probability of satisfying your retirement goals, is determined in large part by the parameters shown in Figure 9.

Figure 9 - Factors that Affect Long-Term Portfolio Accumulation

If at the end of this phase the investor is not on target to meet his retirement date and income goals, little time and few adjustments are available to get back on target. For this reason, this is perhaps the most important of the three life cycle phases.

The length of this period is established by the investor's age at first employment and, since this phase ends five years before retirement, the desired target retirement date. For an academic with several years of post-baccalaureate education, this period is typically 35–40 years in length. These are all critical years, and remember, time goes by fast. It is not unusual for us to meet with individuals who have done little maintenance of their accounts over extended periods of time. I defined earlier the many investment-related risks that you may be exposed to while trying to reach your retirement goals. Another, and perhaps a much more important risk, is the risk associated with no maintenance of your portfolio. This is a risk that you alone can control. Also, don't assume that because you have your assets invested with a certain vendor(s) that those assets are being managed. The investment options you choose are being managed, but not the choice of investment options.

At public universities, academics generally have a choice of a defined benefit or defined contribution retirement plan as their mandatory retirement plan. We believe the choice of a defined benefit plan allows an investor to manage his supplemental plan assets aggressively during this phase. This is true since their mandatory plan assets could be considered a fixed-income investment that will pay a regular reliable monthly benefit.

The savings rate during this phase is an inherently obvious driver that dictates to a large extent the ultimate portfolio value at the end of the long-term phase. Saving could take place in one or more of the supplemental retirement accounts described earlier that provide a tax deferral benefit, or as after-tax savings.

The market risk that you expose yourself to during this phase is a function of your aversion to risk or alternatively the amount of risk that you may need to expose yourself to in order to meet your retirement goals. These variables are manifested by the mix of equity and fixed-income investments in your portfolio and the choice of specific investments within each of these asset groups. It is generally accepted that individuals are rewarded with higher returns as a consequence of their willingness to accept higher levels of risk.

Finally, the variability of equity and fixed-income returns along with the effectiveness of asset management during this period will greatly impact portfolio growth. An investor must in some manner, either by himself or with assistance, manage the portfolio. This process must incorporate a working understanding of the markets, the retirement plans available, the investment choices offered, and the time and inclination to conduct this management. Making ill-informed decisions during any phase of the investment life cycle is a recipe for missing your retirement goals.

Short-Term Accumulation Phase

The short-term accumulation phase is the five-year period immediately preceding retirement. During this period, the investor is normally getting progressively more conservative. There is a school of thought that the percentage of assets invested in fixed-income investments at retirement 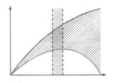 be based upon an individual's age. However, this approach ignores the individual's requirements for income, aversion to risk, and any number of other factors that should influence the allocation of fixed-income investments.

We suggest an approach, shown conceptually in Figure 10, that takes into account the withdrawals and liquidity required by the investor. This approach builds toward having at least five years worth of required distributions from his portfolio in retirement to be invested in various fixed-income investments at the time of retirement. For example, an investor that requires $50,000 in distribution for the five years immediately following his retirement would want to set aside at least $250,000 into fixed-income assets. We attempt to maintain a rolling five years set aside into fixed-income by continually considering the distributions needed over the next subsequent five-year period. Just as important, the investor must invest these fixed-income assets in a manner that incorporates the liquidity required to access these assets as needed.

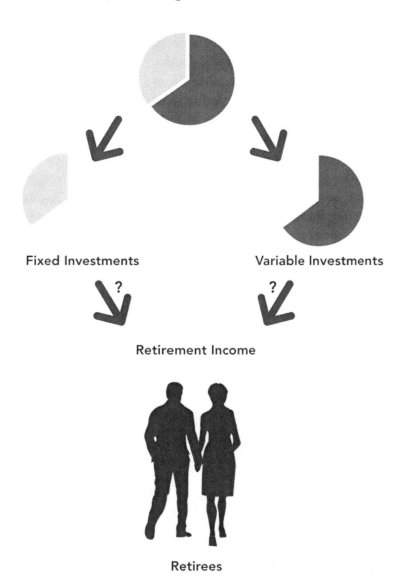

Figure 10 - Planning for Retirement Income
Based on Rolling Five-Year Income Needs

Fixed Investments

Variable Investments

Retirement Income

Retirees

The five years set aside is used because, historically, very few rolling five-year periods have shown a cumulative negative return. Therefore, the five years of retirement income set aside in fixed-income investments is the investor's insurance against having to sell assets in a long-term bear market to fund her retirement.

Following a five-year rolling adjustment to the fixed-income allocation means that four years from retirement at least one year of retirement distributions should be in fixed-income investments, three years from retirement two years of retirement distributions should be in fixed-income investments, and so forth.

The amount of income required in retirement can be estimated by subtracting various payroll deductions (which will be avoided in retirement) from gross salary. These include social security taxes, as well as mandatory and voluntary contributions to university retirement plans. The investor should also incorporate an assumed inflation rate since the goal is to maintain a desired level of purchasing power throughout retirement. The cumulative inflation factor applied will determine the income needed in retirement to maintain the same purchasing power that the investor currently possesses. An example of this approach is shown in Table 4 for an investor who is 53 years old, wishes to retire at his social security full retirement age of 66 years and 6 months, and with an assumed rate of inflation of 2.5 percent. The social security payroll tax is accounted for in this analysis by its two components: Old Age Survivor's and Disability Insurance (OASDI) and Medicare or Hospital Insurance (HI). The inflation factor shown has been computed assuming a compounding of inflation at the rate assumed for the 13 ½ years until his retirement.

Table 4 – Annual Retirement Income Needs Analysis

Gross Annual Wages		**$98,000**
Pre-Tax Contributions		
Mandatory Retirement Plan Contributions	$5,880	
403(b) Plan Contributions	$22,000	
457(b) Plan Contributions	$5,000	
Total Pre-Tax Deductions		**$32,880**
Taxable Income		**$65,120**
Total OASDI/HI Taxes Paid		**$ 7,497**
Disposable Salary		**$57,623**
Cumulative Inflation Factor		**1.40**
Equivalent Retirement Purchasing Power		**$80,421**

The required income level shown in Table 4 is the income needed from all sources. Therefore, the investor's social security benefit, and any defined benefit pension income, should be accounted for by subtracting these income streams from the total income needed in retirement to establish an estimate of the needed withdrawals from the investor's portfolio.

If the investor in this example were to receive an annual social security benefit of $30,000, approximately $50,000 would have to be withdrawn from his retirement portfolio to maintain the same purchasing power in retirement. This investor should then begin positioning his portfolio with the goal of having approximately $250,000 in fixed-income investments upon his retirement. Some may have the luxury of having a total portfolio value that would allow them to be exposed to less risk and therefore have a higher allocation in fixed-income investments.

Others, because of smaller than desired portfolio values, may need to be exposed to slightly higher risk in hopes of achieving a higher overall portfolio return. Still others may simply wish to have a higher amount in fixed-income investments due to their aversion to risk, accepting that lower returns are the cost of less exposure to risk.

Retirement Income Phase

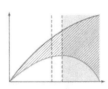

To minimize the likelihood of outliving retirement assets, the retirement income phase should be assumed to extend until the younger spouse reaches the age of 95. This is a conservative condition that, if satisfied, will minimize longevity risk. Portfolio management during this phase of the retirement life cycle is complicated by the need for withdrawals to fund normal retirement income requirements, the uncertainties that may necessitate additional income, and the need to withdraw **required minimum distributions (RMD)** from certain accounts.

> Required minimum distribution: IRS mandated annual withdrawals from retirement accounts based upon the account owner's life expectancy.

There are many factors that will influence how long your retirement portfolio will last. Some of these can be planned for, others obviously cannot. This uncertainty requires investigation of the influence of various parameters on the range of likely outcomes. Because this phase is characterized by the need to take withdrawals from the portfolio, a complicated set of choices must be addressed. These include decisions as to which account within the portfolio to use to fund the distribution, which assets to sell, and when to sell those assets in order to fund the withdrawals needed. Further, if fixed-income assets are periodically used to provide retirement income; one needs to address when to replenish the fixed-income portion of the portfolio. Again, we always strive to have a rainy day fund capable of satisfying income needs for the next five years. In a down stock market, this fund will obviously drop below the five-year level until market conditions allow the fund to be restored.

Once an account is selected for withdrawals, one must choose the specific asset to liquidate in order to fund distributions. This decision should be based on informed and thoughtful criteria. Taking withdrawals pro rata across all assets in an account is a simple but inefficient manner in which to receive retirement income. This is the result that occurs when withdrawals are taken from target retirement date funds.

Investors should apply a reasoned approach to this process by incorporating into the decision recent relative performance and the potential for future returns of each investment. Generally, an investor would want sufficient assets in a money market fund or other highly liquid fixed-income account(s) to provide retirement income for one year. The remainder of the fixed-income portion of the portfolio could be invested in instruments with maturities varying between two and five years. This laddering of maturities of fixed-income assets would allow the investor to maintain sufficient liquidity and to lower his interest rate risk by periodically having "new" money to invest if interest rates are increasing or having monies locked into a higher rate in a declining interest rate environment. A point of emphasis is that the fixed-income assets set aside to protect against selling equity investments in a long-term bear stock market must be available for withdrawal as you may need them.

If the investor owns fixed annuities or stable value funds as part of his fixed-income investments, the restrictions placed upon withdrawals from these accounts must be factored into this process. Also, if bond mutual funds are owned, special attention must be given to the change in market value of the fund that may result in a rising interest rate environment. One must avoid the need to sell these investments during a period when their value may be depressed, just as in the case of equities.

Distributions can be funded from the money market, which is then replenished periodically by efficiently selling equity-based assets. The sale decision is again based on the historical return of different assets and one's sense of potential future returns. This process involves considering these factors not only for fixed-income and equities as a group, but also for each specific holding within these two groups. The negative aspects associated with target retirement date funds described earlier can especially impact the investor during the retirement-income phase, since the target-date approach does not allow the investor to act on this variability in return across asset classes.

Those individuals who have after-tax accounts as a part of their portfolios, either Roth or nonretirement accounts, may be provided other opportunities to better manage taxable income during retirement. Two such approaches are shown conceptually in Figure 11.

Figure 11 - Using After-Tax Assets to Manage Taxable Income

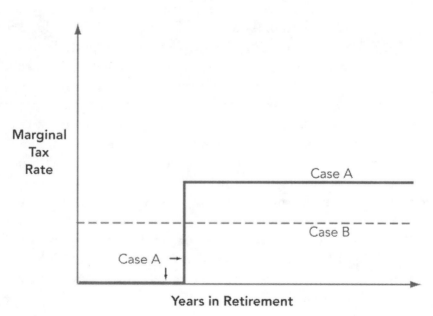

In *Case A*, the investor has chosen to use his after-tax accounts to fully fund his income needs from his portfolio until these assets are depleted. This creates a scenario in which the investor pays little or no taxes for the years during which income is taken only from the after-tax accounts. Once these accounts are depleted, retirement income must then be taken entirely from taxable retirement accounts.

In *Case B* of Figure 11, the investor uses the withdrawals from after-tax accounts to maintain a lower marginal rate than that which would be imposed if all withdrawals were taken from the taxable accounts. In effect, the investor is using smaller withdrawals from the after-tax accounts to lower the average taxes paid over a long period of time.

The best approach for utilizing assets in after-tax accounts will depend upon the following:

> ➤ The percentage of the total portfolio that after-tax assets represent
> ➤ Whether the after-tax accounts are Roth IRAs or nonretirement accounts
> ➤ The tax rate imposed on capital gains and dividends paid in after-tax nonretirement accounts
> ➤ The ability to avoid the taxability of social security benefits by maintaining taxable income below prescribed IRS limits
> ➤ The investor's ability to attain a lower marginal tax rate by using a combination of withdrawals from after-tax accounts and taxable retirement accounts based on income needs and the tax schedules imposed upon them

Some individuals feel that they must purchase a lifetime annuity with certain retirement assets. In this case, the annuity vendor, in return for a fixed amount of assets, provides the purchaser and a second income beneficiary, if selected, an income for life and/or for a certain period. Even though some university employers previously required the immediate **annuitization** of all mandatory plan assets, this is seldom the case any longer.

> Annuitization: The process of converting assets into an income stream through the purchase of an immediate annuity. Various income options can be selected.

Annuitizing assets in this manner does provide the investor with a reliable source of income; however, annuitization can have pitfalls for the investor, including the loss of control of these assets. The amount of income received by the investor is primarily determined by the owner and the income beneficiary's ages and current market interest rates. Insurers use unisex life expectancy tables when computing these income streams for employer-sponsored retirement plan assets. Unisex tables assume equal life expectancies for males and females. Non-employer plans use sex-specific actuarial data which assume a shorter life expectancy for males. Therefore, non-employer accounts such as IRAs that are annuitized, will pay higher incomes to males than if those assets were annuitized while in an employer-sponsored plan. For this reason, males who plan to annuitize some university-sponsored assets might first want to rollover these assets to an IRA before completing the annuitization.

Case Studies

Case Study 1: Make Sure Your Fixed-Income Investments Will Be Available When You Need Them

Scenario: Edith is retiring next month. She knows that she will need $50,000 each year from her retirement accounts to maintain her lifestyle. She currently has $250,000 invested in a single fixed-income account that she set aside two years ago to protect her if a bear market occurs during her retirement. She contacts the vendor of her account to request a distribution and discovers that she is limited to withdrawing $30,000 per year from the $250,000 she has set aside. Further, she is told that in order to get the $30,000 (only 60 percent of what she needs) she must set into motion a payout of the entire balance over no fewer than nine years. Now she is concerned that she may not have access to her fixed-income assets as she needs them.

Solution: Edith has a right to be concerned. If her luck is running bad and there is a long-term bear market, this dilemma could greatly expose her to the risk of outliving her money or force her to lower her standard of living. At this point, Edith has no choice but to start the nine-year payout from her account and hope for the best. It is important to understand the restrictions imposed upon your accounts, the alternatives that are available to you with other vendors, and the opportunities resulting from acting upon a triggering event to gain a higher level of control of your investment choices. Edith could have set the $250,000 aside into a more liquid account with her current vendor or one of the other vendors' products in her retirement plan. At her retirement she could have then performed a rollover of her retirement assets into an IRA that would have provided her with many more options.

Case Study 2: Target Retirement Date Funds Do Not Allow You to Take Advantage of Market Dynamics

Scenario: Woodrow is 42 and busy with research projects and teaching. He has 6th and 8th grade sons at home. He has chosen to invest his retirement assets in a target retirement date fund because of his frenetic lifestyle. He eats lunch most days with a few of his colleagues who periodically talk about selling funds that have done well in the U.S. market so they can reinvest them in foreign funds that have not performed as well, but are priced at what they believe to be good values.

Solution: Since Woodrow is invested in a target date retirement fund, he can't take advantage of the differences in performance between asset classes over time in the same manner that his colleagues can. He has chosen an approach that does not lend itself to portfolio management based upon the dynamics of the market. His only solution is to transition to a managed portfolio of funds distributed across various asset classes. Since he has so many demands upon his time, he may want to begin working with a professional whom he trusts to accomplish this.

Case Study 3: Using After-Tax Assets to Lower Your Taxes in Retirement

Scenario: Hannah is 60, is retiring tomorrow, and will need to start withdrawing money monthly from her investment accounts. She needs $55,000 per year of after-tax money. Most of her portfolio is in three retirement accounts, but approximately 10 percent (roughly $110,000) is in a nonretirement account that was funded by an inheritance. These assets are in a savings account at her credit union. She is trying to decide from which accounts she should withdraw her $55,000 per year. She has decided to withdraw $66,666 per year from her retirement accounts in order to have the $55,000 she will need after-taxes.

Solution: A colleague suggests to Hannah that she may want to consider instead using the after-tax savings account to lower her marginal tax rate by taking just enough from this latter account to avoid receiving income that would be taxed at the 25 percent marginal tax rate. Hannah completes a simplified analysis of these two options, which is summarized below.

Hannah's Tax Schedule

Taxable Income	Tax Rate
$0.00 - $10,000	10%
$10,001 - $45,000	15% of amount > $10,000
$45,001 - $110,000	25% of amount > $45,000

Option 1: Take Income First from After-Tax Account

Year	Retirement Distribution	After-Tax Withdrawal	Taxes Paid	Net
1	0	$55,000	0	$55,000
2	0	$55,000	0	$55,000
3	$66,666	0	$11,666	$55,000
4	$66,666	0	$11,666	$55,000
5	$66,666	0	$11,666	$55,000
6	$66,666	0	$11,666	$55,000
7	$66,666	0	$11,666	$55,000
		Total Taxes Paid	$58,335	

Option 2: Take Only the Amount from After-Tax Account Needed to Reduce Marginal Tax Rate

Year	Retirement Distribution	After-Tax Withdrawal	Taxes Paid	Net
1	$45,000	$16,250	$6,250	$55,000
2	$45,000	$16,250	$6,250	$55,000
3	$45,000	$16,250	$6,250	$55,000
4	$45,000	$16,250	$6,250	$55,000
5	$45,000	$16,250	$6,250	$55,000
6	$45,000	$16,250	$6,250	$55,000
7	$50,000	$12,500	$7,500	$55,000
		Total Taxes Paid	$45,000	

Hannah has determined that her after-tax money will last for seven years if she takes the approach suggested by her colleague. Further, if she takes her colleague's advice, she will save approximately 30 percent in income taxes over this seven-year period by taking this approach rather than the approach she had originally considered.

Case Study 4: Think Twice Before Annuitizing Retirement Assets

Scenario: Martin is retiring next year and is thinking about using the $1,000,000 in his retirement accounts to buy an immediate annuity that will pay him $50,000 per year for life. If he dies before his wife, Ellen, she will receive the same amount until her death. He views managing his accounts as a burden that will prevent him from enjoying his retirement. Martin and Ellen plan on traveling together extensively and enjoying their four grandchildren after he retires.

Solution: Martin and Ellen are taking a risk. If they are unfortunate, and both die prematurely, no one will receive the $50,000 per year after the second spouse dies. In other words, Martin and Ellen plan to give the insurance company $1,000,000 in return for receiving the annual payment. In these circumstances, their children and grandchildren stand to receive none of the money Martin and Ellen have saved if they both die prematurely. Martin and Ellen should consider having all or major portions of their investment portfolio actively managed and perhaps purchase an immediate annuity with only a portion of their assets.

Case Study 5: Avoid Paying Taxes on Your Social Security Benefit in Retirement

Scenario: Julia and John are both at their social security full retirement age and are now retiring from their faculty positions. They have $1,250,000 in various retirement accounts and $250,000 in after-tax assets. They need a total of $100,000 per year in taxable retirement income. Their social security benefit is $40,000 annually. They are trying to determine which accounts they should use to take the remainder of their needed retirement income. They file joint tax returns, so their average tax rate would be 20 percent if their gross taxable income is $100,000.

Solution: Julia and John should take just enough from their retirement accounts to keep their modified adjusted gross income beneath the maximum allowed by the IRS in order to avoid paying federal income taxes on their social security benefit. The additional income needed over and above their social security benefit should be withdrawn from their after-tax assets. This will allow the couple to avoid paying taxes on their social security benefit at least until they must take required minimum distributions from their retirement accounts. Since some of their income will come from after-tax assets and their social security benefit will not be taxed, the sum of their withdrawals from retirement accounts, after-tax accounts, and their social security benefit will be less than the $100,000 of taxable income they would have needed. If their average tax rate would have been 20 percent had they taken their entire portfolio withdrawals from their retirement accounts, they would save $8,000 per year by following this approach and avoiding paying taxes on their social security benefit.

Chapter 6

Factors That Drive the Redesign of the Academic's Portfolio

This chapter describes our firm's approach to:

➤ Assisting clients in establishing reasonable retirement goals
➤ Developing individual investment plans designed to achieve those goals
➤ Implementing the steps to meet those goals
➤ Tracking progress towards achieving those retirement goals
➤ Maintaining procedures to ensure that the client makes those adjustments necessary to meet goals

This chapter also provides insights regarding beneficiary issues and the manner in which certain account types should be managed for tax efficiency. Our approach to retirement planning has been tested with success during a variety of market conditions and for individuals with a range of investment goals, financial circumstances, and risk tolerances.

Establish Investment Goals

Setting retirement goals that include a target retirement date and retirement income is the first step in the retirement planning process. Chapter 5 discussed the process that can be followed in estimating the retirement income needed to maintain the same level of purchasing power as that available during full employment.

We generally want to establish a range of desired retirement income levels that are centered about a target income level. Maximum possible and minimum required income levels are defined in order to provide insight into the range of possible outcomes. This process allows the investor to understand the influence of various factors on these outcomes. Specifically, the following factors are studied through the investment life cycle using retirement projection software:

➢ Mandatory retirement plan contribution rates
➢ Supplemental retirement plan contribution rates
➢ Rate of salary increase
➢ Rate of inflation
➢ Size and start date of other sources of retirement income such as pensions and social security
➢ Allocation between fixed-income and variable assets during each phase of the investment life cycle
➢ Fixed-income and variable returns
➢ Mix of after-tax and retirement assets

You may have specific financial needs that require attention during the development of a retirement plan. These may include evaluating various methods of funding college education for children, choosing among several financing options for large purchases, deciding when to begin social security benefits, or determining the most efficient method of utilizing inheritance assets. The process that we follow with our clients integrates these and other issues into a comprehensive plan that establishes how retirement goals can be met, those factors that are most likely to have the greatest negative impact on reaching these goals, and methods for measuring progress toward meeting these goals.

Determine the Attainability of Retirement Goals

Once target retirement date and income are established, the process of developing a plan to achieve these goals or making needed adjustments begins. We determine the reasonableness of a client's retirement goals by computing the rate of growth and depletion of portfolio assets throughout the investment life cycle. We want our clients to have the confidence that, under assumed reasonable combinations of the factors mentioned in the previous section, the client's assets will last at least until the youngest spouse reaches the age of 95. We accomplish this by completing a series of retirement projections that establish the sensitivity of retirement goals to these previously mentioned factors.

Figure 12 shows conceptually the results of such an analysis for a scenario in which the investor will fall short of meeting her retirement goals. The graph shows changes in total portfolio value during the retirement income phase for three different income levels. Figure 12 assumes that the investor has progressed through the long-term and short-term accumulation periods and has now begun to withdraw retirement income from her portfolio. This analysis assumes a target income level (Itarg), a maximum possible income level (Imax), and a minimum required income level (Imin). In this example, the client has chosen a combination of retirement date and target retirement income level that can't be satisfied by the portfolio assets she will accumulate during her years of service under the assumed market rates of return and planned pattern of savings. Even a minimum income requirement is not sustainable through age 95.

Figure 12 - Retirement Income Sustainability

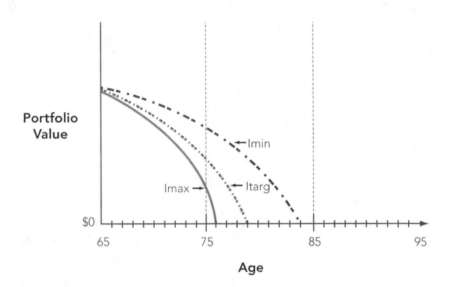

There is a high probability that this individual will outlive her money under this scenario. Because she will probably not meet her goals for target retirement income and/or desired retirement age, she must make changes in some combination of her pattern of savings, level of risk, target retirement income, target retirement date, or she must increase the effectiveness of her portfolio management.

Determine Changes Needed to Meet Retirement Goals

Figure 12 suggests that some combination of this individual's target retirement income, retirement age, savings rate, market risk, or the effectiveness of portfolio management must be modified. Figure 13 shows how affirmative changes in one or more of these factors could allow this individual to satisfy her retirement goals (Ishift) by increasing the portfolio value at the beginning of the retirement income phase and slowing the rate of depletion of assets as withdrawals are made. This shift to a more favorable outcome can be achieved by an appropriate change in any of the previously mentioned factors.

Figure 13 – Enhanced Retirement Income Sustainability

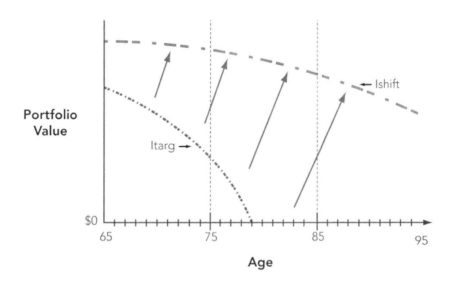

Increasing pre-tax savings is one possible change that could cause a significant improvement in wealth preservation, as could a willingness to accept less retirement income or simply retiring later. Other approaches could include changes in portfolio structure that might expose an investor to more risk in an attempt to achieve higher returns or to implement a plan for more efficiently managing the portfolio. Each investor should complete an evaluation of his portfolio to determine if he is positioned in quality assets. The difference between mediocre and above average performance has historically been significant across all asset classes. This is an extremely significant determinant to the success or failure of your overall strategy.

The investor must become aware of any shortcomings that will prevent him from attaining his goals as early as possible. Recognizing within a few years of retirement that changes must be made limits your options, in many cases to the point that the only parameters that can affect your outcome are reducing your retirement income, postponing your retirement, or some combination of both.

Dealing With Uncertainties in Retirement Planning

It is impossible to plan for the many uncertainties that might occur during an individual's actual progression through the asset accumulation and retirement phases. Unplanned large expenses, health issues, changes in one's financial circumstances that prohibit the ability to make contributions to supplemental plans, and any number of other occurrences can have a negative impact on your well-thought-out plans. These uncertainties can best be addressed by consistently favoring assumptions that tend to underestimate the growth of portfolio assets during the accumulation phases and overestimate the depletion of these assets during the retirement income phase.

An inherent characteristic of investment markets is the uncertainty that accompanies them. The average return of equity investments is a critical factor that dictates to a large extent the success of an investor's retirement plan. However, don't overlook the significance of the sequence of equity returns on the rate of depletion of assets during the retirement income phase. Investors in any phase are vulnerable to the market's volatility, but those in the retirement income phase are even more sensitive to an unfortunate timing of returns. They may retire at a favorable time in the market or during an extremely unfavorable time. Generally, with all other factors being equal, a scenario with negative market returns at the beginning of the retirement income phase will result in a more rapid depletion of assets than one in which the early retirement income years coincide with positive market return. This is true even though the average return throughout the retirement income phase is the same for both scenarios.

The same is true with fixed-income assets that you may own that are subject to interest rate risk. For example, bond funds will have a decrease in market value in rising interest rate environments. The extent of this drop in value will depend primarily upon the average maturity and credit quality of the bonds in the fund. Market valuations of bonds with longer maturities and poorer credit quality will be affected more harshly during periods of rising interest rates.

While there is no way to control the sequence of returns, investors should have a methodology in place to insulate their portfolios from downside risk including an approach to withdrawing income that does not compound this problem by liquidating assets that have seen a decrease in value. This issue highlights the importance of efficiently managing portfolio liquidation to provide retirement income, of making conservative assumptions during retirement planning, and of having sufficient liquidity for fixed-income assets.

Approaches to Withdrawing Retirement Income

There are many approaches that could be followed in selecting the asset to be liquidated to provide your income needs in retirement. Restructuring of your portfolio to consolidate accounts in a manner that gives you a high degree of control over your portfolio is an important step in this process. This methodology must identify the account from which income is to be received, whether to liquidate fixed-income or variable investments, which asset class and specific asset to liquidate, and when and how to replenish the fixed-income investments when these assets decrease below a desired level.

These decisions must consider the tax consequences of withdrawals from specific accounts, RMDs that must be taken, current gains and losses of each holding, the prospect for future gains and losses, and restrictions that might prevent withdrawals from certain accounts. Taking withdrawals pro rata from each holding in an account is not an efficient method to follow. This approach will invariably lead to the liquidation of certain assets that have a better near term potential for gain than other assets. Taking this approach will prevent the investor from taking full advantage of the variability in returns of the fixed-income and equity markets. In the long run, these inefficiencies will lead to a faster depletion of your portfolio assets than if other more reasoned approaches were followed.

The Importance of Getting Your Beneficiaries Correct

Significant complexities and costs to your heirs can be avoided or mitigated by properly designating beneficiaries for both your retirement and nonretirement accounts. Getting this part wrong could force your intended beneficiaries to liquidate assets in a bear market and generate taxable income at significant marginal tax rates. Worse yet, your assets could pass in part or total to unintended individuals.

You should have both primary and contingent beneficiaries designated for retirement accounts. If you have one or more individuals that you want to receive your retirement assets upon your death, they should be specifically named as beneficiaries. One of the common errors that we see prospective clients make is a failure to update their beneficiaries as events occur in their lives. If you intend for individuals to receive the assets in an account if the primary beneficiary predeceases you, you should make sure that those individuals are named as contingent beneficiaries. If the primary beneficiary does not survive the account owner, the contingent beneficiary becomes entitled to the account. The beneficiaries of your retirement accounts should be reviewed periodically to ensure that this designation is consistent with your wishes.

If no beneficiary is named or if the beneficiary has predeceased you, the assets in the account will pass to the estate, resulting in the sale of the assets in the account and payment of income tax on the total value of all of the assets in the account. This would be particularly detrimental if your death were to occur during a bear market, resulting in the forced sale of the assets at depressed prices.

Assets in retirement accounts with named individuals as beneficiaries pass to those individuals and maintain their retirement account status. Although the beneficiary may choose to liquidate all or a portion of the assets, thereby resulting in a taxable event, no assets have to be sold immediately, and there is no immediate tax consequence of the inheritance. The beneficiary will eventually be required to withdraw assets from the account subject to RMD rules. The timing and amount of these required withdrawals will depend upon whether the beneficiary is a spouse or non-spouse and the age of the account owner at his or her death.

Any withdrawals by the beneficiary within the first five years will not be subjected to the 10% early withdrawal penalty normally imposed by the IRS regardless of whether the beneficiary has reached the age of 59 ½. After this initial five-year period, any withdrawals that exceed the RMD will be subject to the 10 percent early withdrawal penalty for a beneficiary who is younger than 59 ½.

Many individuals are not aware that not only can retirement accounts have named beneficiaries, but so can nonretirement accounts. In the latter case, this is as simple as converting the registration of an account from individually or jointly owned to a **Transfer Upon Death** (TOD) **account**.

> Transfer Upon Death account: A type of nonretirement account that has a named beneficiary who will receive the assets in the account upon the account owner's death.

Both individually owned and jointly owned accounts can be changed to TOD accounts. As in the case of retirement accounts, this allows the assets in the account to pass directly to a beneficiary without going through probate. Probate might require the forced sale of the assets and perhaps the assets being distributed in a manner that is inconsistent with your wishes. Brokerage accounts, bank accounts, and individual CDs can each be designated as TOD accounts. Unlike requirements for retirement accounts, the IRS does not impose any withdrawal requirements upon assets that are inherited from a TOD account.

How Tax Rules Can Affect the Management of Certain Accounts

Current tax law provides for favorable tax treatment of dividends and long-term capital gains generated in nonretirement accounts. The tax rates imposed on these proceeds are, in many cases, less than the individual's marginal tax rate. Even more favorable tax treatment is given to Roth accounts in which the growth of the account is not subject to income tax. Although the tax on gains in traditional IRAs and university-sponsored retirement accounts will grow tax-deferred as long as they remain in retirement accounts, they will be taxed as ordinary income when withdrawn. Roth accounts are the exception to this rule, since earnings in these accounts are not taxed if the minimum holding period of five years has been satisfied.

For this reason, one should consider managing Roth accounts and after-tax accounts more aggressively. An investor should make necessary adjustments in other retirement accounts to ensure that the total portfolio is managed consistent with his overall investment objective by conservatively managing a portion of his retirement assets to balance the changes made in the Roth and nonretirement accounts. This provides further rationale for managing your assets as a total cohesive portfolio.

In this manner, the portfolio has the balance between fixed-income and equity investments to match your risk tolerance, while individual accounts are managed to take advantage of the investment options and tax benefits available to that account.

Case Studies

Case Study 1: A Bear Market Has Created Buying Opportunities

Scenario: William is 45 and is fairly risk averse with only 35 percent of his retirement assets invested in equity-based mutual funds. He began saving later than most of his colleagues because of a two-year post-doctoral position and only began contributing to his supplemental 403(b) two years ago. He now sees the benefit of this pretax savings and intends to continue contributing the maximum amount. The stock market has just dropped by 40 percent, which makes William even more risk averse and makes him even more inclined to continue investing primarily in fixed-income investments. However, when he completes an analysis of his retirement years he can only see his retirement assets lasting from retirement at age 65 until he is 80 years old.

Solution: William is in that age group for which it could be argued that the recent drop in the stock market is a good thing. William will be putting more money into his retirement plans in the future than he has saved in those plans up until this point in his life. If the market has dropped by 40 percent, it will increase by 67 percent from this point if it recovers to its pre-collapse level, even if that recovery takes 10 years. William should strongly consider exposing himself to more market risk by increasing his allocation to equity investments, but more importantly, he should strive to manage his portfolio more efficiently.

Case Study 2: Lower the Risk of Outliving Your Money

Scenario: Anna is 60 and is planning for her retirement in five years. She feels confident that her assets will last until she is 85 and that she will therefore have sufficient retirement assets to retire comfortably. She is basing this conclusion on an analysis that she completed in which she assumed that her equity-based returns would average 10 percent per year during retirement.

Solution: Anna has taken a fairly liberal approach to retirement planning and should consider making a more conservative projection by stretching her life expectancy to age 95. Hopefully, Anna will live well beyond the age of 85, but even if she does not, the assumption of a 10 percent average stock market return may also be an aggressive assumption. The market may indeed return 10 percent per year, but the sequence of returns is a significant factor that will influence the depletion of her retirement assets. Extending her life expectancy for the purpose of her retirement projection is a more conservative approach that will provide an offsetting influence to the uncertainties created by not knowing in advance what the sequence of market returns will actually be during her retirement.

Case Study 3: Get Your Beneficiary Designations Correct and Save Your Heirs Taxes, Trouble, and Market Losses

Scenario: Andrew and his wife Eliza have two children in college and have named each other as the primary beneficiary of each of their retirement accounts, but no contingent beneficiaries have been named. They also have a joint brokerage account and several CDs at two banks. Andrew owns some of the CDs individually, and Eliza owns others. The maturities vary from three months to five years. They feel as though since each owns a portion of the CDs, upon the death of either, the remaining spouse would have access to the cash necessary to fund any short-term expenses that might occur.

Solution: Andrew and Eliza have done half the job of planning for their heirs. Should the couple have the misfortune of dying in the same accident or if one predeceases the other and the surviving spouse fails to update beneficiary designations, their children may have some inheritance problems. They should name their children as contingent beneficiaries on the retirement accounts, convert the brokerage account to a TOD account while naming the children as beneficiary, and finally they should reregister the CDs to be jointly owned in a TOD account and name the children as the beneficiaries of those accounts.

Case Study 4: After-Tax Accounts Should Be Weighted Towards Growth

Scenario: Louisa is 54 years old and is recently divorced. She currently has $160,000 in various retirement accounts and $140,000 in a nonretirement brokerage account. She has set aside sufficient assets in a bank savings account to get her through any unplanned major expense. Louisa considers the assets in her nonretirement account as "retirement" assets that will be used to partially fund the income she will need after she retires. She plans to continue working until she reaches her full social security retirement age of 66 years and 2 months. Louisa has roughly 60 percent of the assets in her nonretirement account invested in a mix of corporate bonds, CDs, and money market funds, and the remainder in individual stocks. The assets in her retirement accounts are primarily in equity-based mutual funds that are split between foreign and U.S. funds.

Solution: Louisa should reverse her allocation so that her nonretirement account contains most of the growth portion of her portfolio, and the retirement accounts have the fixed-income portion that she desires in her portfolio. This will allow her to take advantage of the favorable tax treatment of long-term capital gains and qualified dividends while moving the more conservative (and presumably slower growing) assets into her retirement accounts that will eventually be taxed at her ordinary income tax rate. This allows her the advantage of tax deferral on interest income. Louisa will not receive this benefit if she leaves the interest bearing investments in her nonretirement account, since interest in these types of accounts is taxed at normal income tax rates when it is earned regardless of when the interest is withdrawn from the account.

Chapter 7

Restructuring and Managing Academics' Portfolios

This chapter pulls together the various concepts introduced previously to show how sound portfolios can be designed and managed in a way that increases the probability that retirement goals will be met. This process requires that the investor:

➢ take those steps necessary to complete the various rollovers and transfers required to convey the highest degree of investment flexibility and control

➢ reallocate the assets within the portfolio consistent with your investment objective, account constraints, and current financial situation

➢ continually monitor performance of holdings within the portfolio

➢ make adjustments as needed to reflect the changing financial environment

➢ effectively incorporate changes in university-sponsored plans

➢ make those modifications dictated by progression through the investment life cycle

Restructure Portfolio to Gain Better Control

Investors should complete a critical review of their existing accounts and continue through a series of steps aimed at better positioning their assets. Where there are no overriding issues to the contrary, investors should first make use of triggering events that will allow university-sponsored assets to be rolled over into an IRA. Second, investors should determine if it is in their best interest to complete an intraplan transfer that would replace a vendor or to use a second vendor to expand the number of investment options beyond that provided by a current vendor. The following steps provide a summary of the process that investors should follow:

> ➢ Step 1 – Establish the strengths and weaknesses of existing accounts and other accounts that are available as a result of triggering events that have been satisfied.
> ➢ Step 2 – Establish the desired fixed-income and variable investment allocation.
> ➢ Step 3 – Determine liquidity needs from fixed-income investments.
> ➢ Step 4 – Identify those accounts that allow fixed-income investments that satisfy your risk, return, and liquidity needs.

Figure 14 shows an example of how portfolios could be restructured to gain better control and to expand available investment options that might allow for a more efficient management of portfolio assets. In this example, an individual has a single ORP account with one of four available vendors in the university's plan, a 403(b) account with his current university employer, two accounts with a previous university employer, and a traditional IRA.

Figure 14 - Sample Portfolio Redesign

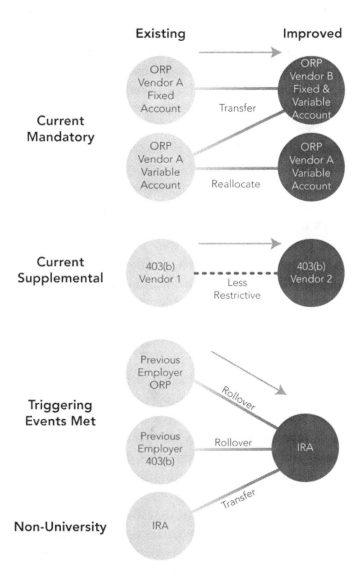

This investor's most restrictive account is her mandatory retirement plan. She is an employee at a public university and has chosen the defined contribution plan, or ORP in this case, as her mandatory plan. She has a single ORP vendor through this current employer and has both variable and fixed-income accounts with that vendor. The investor wants to retain some of her variable assets with Vendor A, but sees the benefit of opening a second ORP account with Vendor B in order to expand the investment options available. An intraplan transfer to Vendor B of a portion of the variable ORP assets is completed to satisfy this objective. The investor has also chosen to redirect her monthly ORP contributions to Vendor B. These contributions can be redirected to another vendor at a later time if the investor wishes.

The ORP vendor has placed the fixed-income assets in a separate account from the variable assets. The investor is close enough to retirement that she needs to begin the process of increasing the liquidity of those fixed-income assets. Most vendors impose restrictions on withdrawals from fixed-income accounts. Some vendors remove these restrictions upon satisfaction of certain triggering events such as separation from service. Vendor A imposes restrictions upon withdrawals from the fixed-income portion that require that withdrawals be made in no fewer than 10 equal payments over a nine-year period. In this case, the investor has chosen to instruct Vendor A to transfer these annual payments to one or more of the variable accounts with Vendor B. Since the investor is still employed with the university at which this account was established, these payments must remain with one of the vendors in the ORP of that university.

If the investor wishes to have those transfers invested in non-equity investments, she could reinvest the proceeds into one or more bond or money market funds. However, the investor now has the flexibility, if she wishes, to reinvest those assets into an equity-based mutual fund with Vendor B and take a similar amount in her IRA and invest that into a corporate bond, CD, or some other fixed-income instrument that is now available to her in that very accommodating IRA account.

The next least restrictive account that the investor has is the 403(b) account with Vendor 1 that she is currently contributing to. She has concluded that Vendor 2 is better able to meet her investment objectives so she has decided to complete an intraplan transfer to Vendor 2 and to begin making her monthly contributions to this new account.

Since both the ORP and 403(b) changes involve intraplan transfers, these must be completed as trustee-to-trustee transfers, and the investor will never be in receipt of the funds. As in the case of the rollovers and transfer into the IRA, these intraplan transfers are nontaxable events.

This investor has the most flexibility with those accounts that have satisfied various triggering events. In this case, since she has terminated employment with a previous employer, she can rollover her two previous university plans into an IRA. She decides to move both of these two accounts and her IRA into a single **brokerage IRA.** Movement of the assets in the existing IRA is completed by an electronic **in-kind transfer**.

Brokerage IRA: A type of IRA that grants the investor the greatest degree of control over the investment options that may be used. The account is established directly with a brokerage firm.

In-Kind transfer: A type of transfer from one account to another in which the shares of the holdings in an account are transferred electronically between trustees without the sale of assets.

Since the two previous university plans are employer-sponsored plans, moving these assets into an IRA requires that a rollover be completed. For rollovers, assets must be sold and the proceeds mailed or sent electronically to the trustee of the brokerage IRA. All three of these transactions are nontaxable events. If, however, for some reason the investor comes into possession of the assets, she must be sure to forward the funds to the new custodian within 60 days of receipt.

The investor now has restructured her portfolio in a manner that provides for a broader selection of investment options, reduces the number of custodians that she must deal with, gives her a higher level of control over her fixed-income options, and potentially exposes her to less risk and higher returns.

Make Initial Purchases and Exchanges

Once all transfers and rollovers are complete, the process of reinvesting the assets begins. The following steps should be followed during the process of reallocating investments.

➢ Step 1 – Establish desired allocation between foreign and U.S. equity investments.

➢ Step 2 – Establish country- or region-specific focus for foreign funds.

➢ Step 3 – Establish asset class diversification for U.S. equity investments.

➢ Step 4 – Determine appropriate fixed-income investments and identify accounts into which these instruments can be purchased.

➢ Step 5 - Proceed to reinvest assets starting with the most restrictive accounts and progressing to those with the least restrictions.

The strengths of each account might lie in the specific investments available subject to the restrictions imposed, as is the case with the ORP account, or the flexibility to invest in a wide variety of investments such as in a brokerage IRA. The IRS restricts the investment options available in 403(b), 401(k), and 457(b) accounts. Individual bonds and CDs are not available in any of these university plans but are available in brokerage IRAs. Therefore, if there is a desire to own these instruments, they will need to be obtained in the IRA. This option is of increased importance during the retirement income phase when the requirement for liquidity and control of these assets is paramount because of the need for withdrawals and to hedge against market risk.

The ORP vendors available to the investor may each offer only one fund within each asset class. The product offered by ORP Vendor A may have strengths in large cap funds while the strength of the product offered by ORP Vendor B might lie in the foreign funds available. This does not mean that the large cap funds available through Vendor A or the foreign funds provided by Vendor B are better than the universe of funds of that type available in the brokerage IRA, but simply that they are the best available from various ORP vendors. In the same manner, the strength of the funds offered by 403(b) Vendor 2 may be small cap funds. Again, this is the rationale for taking an independent approach with no inherent conflict of interest that would lead you to favor one vendor over another.

In summary, select the best option available subject to the investment restrictions imposed by each university-sponsored plan and the vendor(s) within each plan. This process will in all probability result in a concentration of certain asset classes in specific accounts and in no exposure to specific asset classes in other accounts. In the above example, mid cap funds offered by the two ORP providers may be inferior to those that could be obtained in either the 403(b) or IRA. This could result in having the bulk of the ORP assets concentrated perhaps in only a small number of funds. The assets in the IRA can then be used to fill in the gaps exposed by the limited choices in the ORP and to a lesser extent in the 403(b).

This same logic should be applied for the fixed-income allocation as well. We have shown in Figure 14 a case in which the investor has chosen to begin the process of transferring fixed-income assets out of the account held at Vendor A. If you are 10 years or more from retirement, you might choose not to start these withdrawals at this time if the interest rate offered is better than that which could be obtained in other accounts. However, one must evaluate this possible strength in light of the possible weakness that this rate could change and leave you locked into a long-term contract at a rate that is not competitive with other available options. Additionally, one must consider the advantage of using other fixed-income investments that would convey better control of these assets so that the investor can react efficiently to changes in market interest rates. For those that recognize this need, or that require more liquidity, a choice might be made to invest fixed-income assets in short-term bonds, CDs, and money market funds in their IRA.

Many individuals see the usefulness of investing in targeted investments in sector mutual funds and ETFs. These instruments are seldom made available in ORP accounts but are sometimes available in a limited manner in 403(b) accounts. However, a large selection of sector funds and ETFs are available in brokerage accounts. Another preference for many investors is socially conscious investing, which includes the growing interest in "green" investing. These kinds of funds are available on a very limited basis in university-sponsored plans. There is a much broader selection available in IRA and after-tax brokerage accounts.

After completing this reallocation process, the various accounts in this investor's portfolio might be allocated as shown below:

ORP Accounts

    Vendor A

        Fixed Account

        Large Cap Growth Funds

        Large Cap Value Funds

    Vendor B

        Emerging Markets Funds

        Diversified International Funds

        Canada Fund

403(b) Account

        Small Cap Growth Funds

        Small Cap Value Funds

IRA

        Short-Term Corporate Bonds

        FDIC-Insured CDs

        Mid Cap Growth Funds

        Mid Cap Value Funds

        Sector and Exchange Traded Funds

Monitor Markets and Holdings for Needed Portfolio Changes

It is essential that a consistent set of criteria be employed upon which to base purchase and sell decisions. Some of these criteria are quantitative, while others are qualitative. For mutual funds and exchange traded funds, we collapse several criteria into action signals. These include performance-based criteria that consider short-term and long-term performance compared to all funds with the same investment objective. Qualitative criteria such as the tenure of the fund manager, recent changes in investment objective, portfolio composition, and the size of the fund are also included in the analysis. These criteria are used to assign an action to each fund. These include:

Buy – Fund should be purchased.

Watch Buy – Fund should be monitored closely for possible action to buy.

Hold – No action.

Watch Sell – Fund should be monitored closely for possible action to sell.

Sell – Fund should be sold.

Although fund expenses are a consideration for many when evaluating diversified mutual funds, we do not feel that these expenses are a primary determinant that should dictate purchase and sell decisions. This is because fund expenses are merely part of a balance sheet that factors into the bottom line. In essence, it is not what the investor pays, but more important it is what the investor gets paid in fund return that is of overriding importance. Again, we are more concerned with net returns than trying to find funds with the lowest expenses.

Sector mutual funds, ETFs, and individual stocks must be judged in a somewhat different light than diversified mutual funds that react more slowly to changes in market conditions. Because they are more volatile than diversified mutual funds, these investments require an additional set of criteria. There are times when we will see that our best judgments, and therefore our expectations for an investment, do not turn out the way we planned. These instances should be quickly acknowledged and appropriate changes made. There are also times when we should take profits and not extrapolate returns and expect increasingly higher profits.

Making informed choices when investing is obviously critical to the performance of your portfolio. For example, there is considerable variability in return between diversified mutual fund asset classes over various time intervals and a wide range of returns within each asset class. It is imperative that someone, either the investor or a professional whom the investor trusts, actively manage the portfolio. As an example, the difference in performance between a fund that is in the upper 25th percentile in return and a fund in the 75th percentile could easily be 2 percent to 3 percent annually. Those kinds of performance differences over a 10-year period would make a cumulative difference of 22 percent to 35 percent in return to the investor. Performance differences between equity asset classes, as shown in Figure 3, could easily be 20 percent to 30 percent or more each year. Of course, only a portion of your equity investments would be invested in each asset class due to the need for diversification, so this kind of disparity would only apply to a share of your total equity investments. There are also choices that can be made with fixed-income assets that can improve an investor's return on that component of her portfolio. Many other ideas that have been presented in this and other chapters such as making use of tax or withdrawal efficiencies can improve portfolio performance as well.

Good ideas and watchful oversight of your portfolio could easily capture some of these efficiencies in a manner that could allow you to meet or exceed your retirement goals. Figure 15 shows how improved performance could have positive effects upon an investor's portfolio. The graph shows the effect of an improvement in equity performance from 7.5 percent to 9 percent annually and of fixed-income investments from 4.5 percent to 5.25 percent throughout the investment life cycle. These are modest and achievable improvements if a portfolio is actively and efficiently managed. The investor in this example is assumed to be 50 years old and plans to retire at his social security full retirement age of 66. Other assumptions include the following:

Current Salary – $100,000
Rate of Salary Increase – 2.5%
Rate of Contribution to Mandatory Plan – 12.84% of Salary
Annual Contribution to Supplemental Plans – $0.0
Annual Rate of Inflation – 2.5%
Annual Social Security Benefit – $35,000
Annual Income Needed In Retirement – $120,000
Long-term Accumulation Fixed-Income Allocation – 10%
Short-term Accumulation Fixed-Income Allocation – 20%
Retirement Income Period Fixed-Income Allocation – 35%

This modest improvement in performance can make the difference between this investor fully depleting his assets at the age of 85 or having close to $500,000 remaining at the age of 95.

Figure 15 - Effects of Enhanced Performance on Portfolio Value

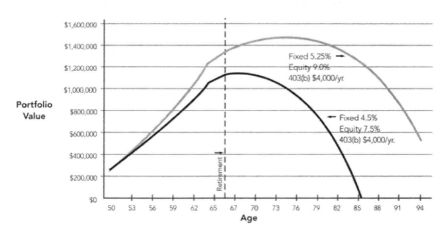

Alternatively, Figure 16 considers this same investor and shows the additional amount of annual retirement contributions that would be needed to offset inferior performance and have the same level of assets that would be available at 95 for the case in which superior performance had been achieved. A total of $14,500 more in annual contributions would be required throughout this individual's investment life cycle to overcome the inferior performance. This would therefore require a cumulative total of $232,000 more in contributions than in the case with enhanced performance.

Figure 16 - Increased Contributions Required to Offset Underperformance of Assets

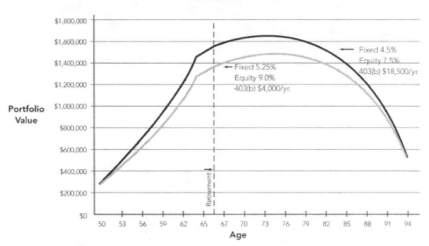

Consequently, what might be perceived as small differences in portfolio performance can have a significant impact on portfolio values over time, the requirement for increased retirement savings, and ultimately the probability of meeting your retirement goals. Improved management can make a significant difference.

Monitor IRS and Plan Changes

The IRS is constantly reviewing and changing various rules that govern university retirement plans. You must be attuned to these changes and take those actions allowable to adapt. This may involve changes in contribution limits, rules that modify the responsibilities of the plan fiduciary, or changes in withdrawal rules. The extensive rule changes for 403(b) accounts that have taken place over the last two years have both created flexibilities and imposed additional constraints on plan participants. The participant can no longer complete transfers to 403(b) vendors that are not part of the university's plan. More stringent requirements imposed by the IRS on plan vendors have caused many to abandon this line of business completely. Also, the more stringent rules imposed on university employers have caused many to dramatically reduce the number of vendors in their plan.

Recent rule changes also now allow all or a portion of 403(b) and 401(k) contributions to be earmarked as after-tax Roth contributions. This has allowed participants to make Roth contributions without being subject to maximum income limits imposed on Roth IRA contributions. In a related rule change, the IRS has removed the income limit on the conversion of Roth accounts to traditional IRAs for calendar year 2010. Also, an exception has been made during that year that allows income taxes due on the converted amount to be spread out over a two-year period instead of being payable in the year of the conversion. Because of the recent downturn in the market and the significant decrease in account values that have occurred, this may be an opportune time to convert traditional IRAs to Roth IRAs. Even though taxes would be due on the value converted, the profits in the account resulting from the recovery of the market would not be taxable.

Changes in investment options in mandatory and supplemental plans that result in the addition and deletion of investment options occur frequently. The investor should make note of these changes but also perform due diligence to evaluate options that have been added to the plan.

Ongoing IRS and plan level changes result in an evolutionary process that must be continually monitored to identify appropriate measures to be taken. Only in this way can the investor make full use of the benefits that these plans convey.

Case Studies

Case Study 1: Gain Control of Your Fixed-Income Investments as You Near Retirement

Scenario: Rachel is 55 years old. She has been with her current employer for five years and has 20 years of previous employment with two different universities. During her time at her two previous faculty positions, she accumulated four retirement accounts. One of these accounts has a fixed-income component worth $200,000, which is equivalent to approximately three times the annual income she will need in retirement. The $200,000 can't be withdrawn in less than nine years due to the vendor's restrictions, regardless of when she requests these funds. She also has a mandatory retirement plan and a supplemental 403(b) with her current employer. Rachel is looking forward to her retirement in 10 years and wants to begin the process of restructuring her portfolio so that she can have complete control over the fixed-income assets in her portfolio at the time of her retirement.

Solution: Unless there are compelling reasons to the contrary, Rachel should rollover the accounts that she accumulated at her previous employers into a single brokerage IRA. She should also begin the nine-year process of rolling over the assets in her fixed-income account to her IRA. She will have a real liquidity problem if she takes no action now. As these annual payments are deposited into her IRA, she could invest the cash into a mix of high quality corporate bonds and CDs that mature in less than 15 years. Over the next 10 years she can use the remainder of the assets in her IRA, which will be increased when she rolls over her 403(b) at age 59 ½, to increase her fixed-income allocation to a level that will allow her to achieve her desired allocation to fixed-income investments at retirement.

Case Study 2: Be Aware of the Volatility Inherent in Bond Funds

Scenario: Andrew is 62 years old with two years of retirement income invested in bond funds in his mandatory retirement plan. He also has a large IRA that resulted from the rollover of his previous employer accounts. Andrew anticipates that interest rates will rise over the next three years and is wondering what strategies he should take to position his portfolio for retirement.

Solution: If interest rates do increase, the market value of his bond funds will likely decrease. Andrew should consider selling his bond funds in his mandatory plan and investing the same amount in fixed-income investments in his IRA. If Andrew invests in relatively short-term corporate bonds of varying maturities, he can reinvest at a higher interest rate when these bonds mature. He could also purchase several FDIC-insured CDs and ladder their maturities. Andrew should consider concentrating his fixed-income investments in his IRA as he progresses towards retirement, since he will have more options in this account and can better manage the liquidity that he will need during retirement.

Case Study 3: Use Previous Employer Accounts to Broaden Your Choices of Socially Conscious Investments

Scenario: James has restructured his portfolio and wants to invest some assets in socially conscious mutual funds. He realized upon investigation that only one is available in the university's mandatory plan. He is 60 and has a 403(b) with his current university's plan and two accounts with a previous university employer.

Solution: James should rollover both accounts with his previous university employer as well as his 403(b) into a single brokerage IRA account. This will allow him access to a wide variety of funds that meet his investment objective. He will be able to find socially conscious funds that span the various asset classes for diversified mutual funds, which are invested in both U.S. and foreign stocks, and will not have to settle for only a single large cap socially conscious fund. He will also be able to invest in the growing number of "green funds" that are now available.

Case Study 4: Concentrate Your Investments First Into the Best Funds Offered Within Your Most Restrictive Plan

Scenario: Sarah is 55 and has a mandatory ORP and a 457(b) account with her current employer. She also has retirement accounts with a previous employer. All of her accounts are with the same vendor.

She wants to maintain her ORP account with this vendor, but she knows that her vendor's best funds are large-cap value and large-cap growth funds. She is aware that the vendor's mid cap, small cap, and foreign funds are inferior with a long history of subpar performance. Sarah does not know how to diversify her portfolio with the single vendor that she has.

Solution: Since Sarah is still employed with her current employer and is not yet 59 ½, she has not satisfied a triggering event that would allow her to rollover the assets in her current employer's plans. Sarah could investigate the investments offered by other vendors in her current university's retirement plans or perhaps a better solution would be to rollover the assets in the retirement accounts she has in her previous university employer's plans. She could then concentrate her investments in her current employer's plans with her vendor's strength, which is the management of large cap funds, and use the assets in her IRA to complement those investments by concentrating investments in her IRA into mid cap, small cap, and foreign funds. This would also allow her to start positioning her fixed-income assets into her IRA as well.

Case Study 5: Attain Your Retirement Goals by Improving the Performance of Your Portfolio

Scenario: Dwight is 45 years old and has $150,000 in retirement assets. He wants to retire at his full retirement age for social security of 66 years and 10 months. His hope is to be able to withdraw an amount from his portfolio that, including his social security benefit, will equal 110% of his current salary. With his busy schedule at work and the demands on his time at home, he has not been able to actively manage these accounts. As a result, he has decided to simply invest half of his assets in fixed-income investments and intends to continue with that allocation through retirement. He completes an analysis of the remainder of his employment years and into his retirement and determines that under his assumed conditions, he will run out of money at the age of 84. The assumptions he makes are as follows:

Current Salary – $80,000
Rate of Salary Increase – 2.5%
Rate of Contribution to Mandatory Plan – 12.84% of Salary
Annual Contribution to Supplemental Plans – $4,000
Annual Rate of Inflation – 2.5%
Annual Social Security Benefit – $25,000
Annual Income Needed In Retirement – $120,000
Return on Fixed-Income Investments – 5.0%
Return on Equity Investments – 7.0%

His wife Mamie is convinced that if his accounts are more diligently managed, he could accept the risk of investing a higher percentage of assets into equity investments. As a result she and Dwight could potentially achieve a higher return and as a result extend the time that his retirement assets will last.

Solution: No one can guarantee that higher returns will result from positioning a higher percentage of assets into equity investments and allocating more time to the management of his assets. But improved long-term performance is probably not going to result from a lack of attention. Dwight changes his assumptions of allocation to fixed-income investments to 10 percent in long-term accumulation, 20 percent in short-term accumulation, and 35 percent in the retirement income phase. He then generates the graph shown in Figure 17 that shows that under these new assumptions, his retirement assets will last until age 93.

Figure 17 - Effect of Fixed-Income and Equity Allocation on Portfolio Value

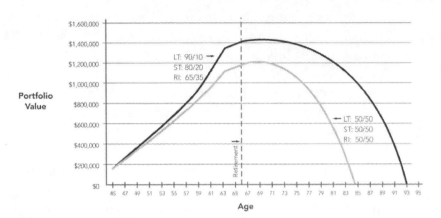

Case Study 6: Use After-Tax Assets to Avoid Paying Taxes on Your Social Security Benefit

Scenario: Michelle currently has $160,000 in various retirement accounts and $140,000 in an after-tax account that she received in an inheritance. She is 54 years old and raising a teenage child, which prevents her from making supplemental retirement plan contributions for the foreseeable future. She believes she will need just over $100,000 of before-tax income from all sources if she retires at her full social security retirement age. She is concerned that she may not be on target to meet her retirement goals.

Solution: If Michelle uses her after-tax assets wisely, she will greatly increase her ability to meet her goals. Michelle's average tax rate is 20 percent, which means that $80,000 of after-tax money is equivalent to $100,000 of before-tax money. If Michelle plans to take her withdrawal from her after-tax account until those assets are depleted, she will also avoid having to pay taxes on her social security benefit. The net result of this approach would be that she would only need to withdraw approximately $50,000 from her after-tax account in order to satisfy her income needs. She now has the $80,000 of after-tax income she needs ($30,000 from social security and $50,000 from her after-tax account) and can now follow this approach until her after-tax assets are depleted. This will also allow her to manage her retirement assets more for growth for an additional six years since she has delayed the need for withdrawals from those accounts. She will be able to continue deferring taxes on her retirement assets until she must first take her RMD and then use these assets to provide for her income needs. Figure 18 shows this approach graphically.

Figure 18 - Change in Portfolio Value Over Time

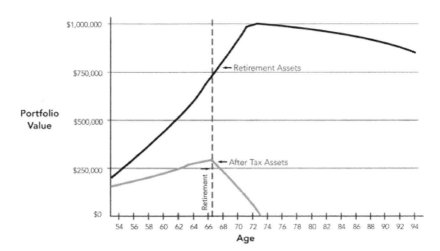

Glossary

Account: A vehicle that allows for investing, including the purchase, sale, and holding of assets with a given vendor.

After-tax assets: Assets for which ordinary income taxes have been previously paid.

After-tax contributions: Monies contributed to an account on which taxes have previously been paid.

Annuities: Investment contracts offered by life insurance companies that provide tax deferral of earnings. Annuities are sold in units, not shares. Annuity contracts have two phases, the accumulation phase (deferred contract) and the payout phase (annuitized contract). Most deferred contracts allow flexible distributions. If annuitized, contracts set forth the terms of paying out the proceeds of the contract with little, if any, flexibility after the initiation of payments.

Annuitization: The process of converting assets into an income stream through the purchase of an immediate annuity. Various income options can be selected.

Asset class: The combination of market capitalization and investment style.

Before-tax contributions: The portion of an employee's salary contributed to a retirement plan before federal income taxes are deducted, resulting in a reduction in the individual's gross income for federal and state tax purposes.

Brokerage IRA: A type of IRA that grants the investor the greatest degree of control over the investment options that may be used. The account is established directly with a brokerage firm.

Capitalization: The total market value of a company, calculated by multiplying the company's outstanding shares by the current share price.

Closed-end mutual fund: A fund company that issues and trades shares like any other corporation and usually does not redeem its shares. These funds are a collection of stocks and/or bonds and may trade at a premium or a discount to its intrinsic value.

Credit risk: Risk of loss of principal due to the default of the issuer.

Credit quality: A measure of a bond issuer's ability to pay interest and principal in a timely manner.

Defined benefit retirement plan: Retirement plan for which the benefits are based on years of service, salary, actuarial factors, and income payment option selected. These are sometimes called pensions and require little employee involvement until retirement, when the retiree determines how he or she would like to receive disbursement.

Defined contribution retirement plan: Retirement plan for which the retirement benefit (i.e., the payout) will depend on several factors including how well the investments have performed over time, age at retirement, and cumulative amount of contributions.

Distributions: The payment of funds from a retirement or pension plan.

Diversified mutual fund: An investment vehicle designed to reduce exposure to risk by diversifying among many publicly traded companies and several industries.

Equity-based investments: Funds invested primarily in common or preferred stock of a company.

Exchange traded fund: A collection of assets such as stocks and bonds that trade continuously during the day in the same manner as individual stocks. These instruments are usually designed to track some broad market, industry, or commodity specific index.

Fiduciary: A person who is vested with legal rights and powers to be exercised for the benefit of another person.

Fixed-income investments: Bonds, money market funds, fixed annuities, and stable value funds that pay a specific rate of interest.

Growth funds: Investment vehicles designed to provide shareholders with growth of capital by investing in companies with a history of rapidly growing earnings and generally higher price-to-earnings ratios. Growth funds are generally more volatile than value funds, rising faster in bull markets and dropping more sharply in bear markets.

Inflation risk: Risk that your assets will not grow at a rate sufficient to maintain purchasing power.

In-kind transfer: A type of transfer from one account to another in which the shares of the holdings in an account are transferred electronically between trustees without the sale of assets.

Investment advisory services: The development and implementation of individual investment plans along with the ongoing supervisory management of investment assets according to this plan.

Investment style: Established by the types of stock; value, or growth held in a fund.

Liquidity: The ability to buy or sell an asset quickly without substantially affecting the asset's price.

Longevity risk: Risk that you and/or your spouse may outlive your assets.

Management expense: A charge paid to a mutual fund's investment adviser for its services. The annual fee is disclosed in each fund prospectus and is typically between 0.5 percent and 2.5 percent.

Mandatory retirement plans: A retirement account for which participation is a condition of employment.

Market risk: Risk of loss due to a decline in the overall market.

Maturity: The date when a debt becomes due for payment. A bond due to mature on June 1, 2015, will return the bondholder's principal and final interest payment on that date.

Money market mutual funds: Funds that hold short-term debt securities, such as commercial paper, certificates of deposit, and treasury bills, with a maturity of one year or less. Typically, these are safe, highly liquid investments.

Mutual fund: A fund operated by an investment company that invests in one or more categories of assets, including stocks, bonds, real estate, commodities, money market instruments, etc.

Open-end mutual fund: A fund operated by an investment company that invests in one or more categories of assets, including stocks, bonds, and money market instruments. Investors can redeem mutual fund shares on demand. Mutual funds offer investors diversification and professional money management. A management fee is charged for these services, and there may be other expenses. Funds with a sales charge are called load funds, while those sold without commission are called no-load funds.

Plan document: The document that describes the various rules which govern an employer-sponsored retirement plan. This document is created and, when necessary, amended by the plan sponsor.

Plan sponsor: An organization or entity that offers a retirement plan to an employee group. In the case of a plan maintained by a single employer, the plan sponsor is generally the employer. In the case of a plan maintained by one or more employers or organizations, the plan sponsor is the association, committee, joint board of trustees or other similar group of representatives of the parties involved.

Portfolio: The collection of accounts that encompasses all of your invested assets.

Registered investment advisory: A firm that manages the investments of others. The firm is regulated by the firm's state of residency or the Securities and Exchange Commission, depending on the level of assets under management

Required minimum distribution: IRS mandated annual withdrawals from retirement accounts based upon the account owner's life expectancy.

Retirement assets: Assets that are anticipated to be used to produce retirement income.

Rollover: A tax-free reinvestment of a distribution from a retirement plan into an IRA or other qualified plan, providing the reinvestment is completed within 60 days of the distribution.

Sector mutual fund: A mutual fund that concentrates on a relatively narrow market sector (such as utilities or technology companies). These funds can experience higher price volatility than a diversified fund.

Stable value accounts of annuities: Accounts that seek to preserve principal and pay current interest rates. These are similar to fixed annuities. They usually offer few if any guarantees but also have fewer withdrawal restrictions.

Stockbroker: A regulated professional who buys and sells securities based upon a client's instructions and generally receives a commission for completing the transaction.

Subaccount: The various investment options within an annuity product.

Supplemental retirement plan: A voluntary plan that allows employees to make contributions, over and above mandatory contributions, via payroll deductions; these include 403(b), 401(k), and 457(b) plans.

Target retirement date mutual funds: Mutual funds with an asset allocation mix among stocks, bonds, and short-term instruments that are more aggressive for younger investors and become more conservative as investors approach retirement.

Transfer: Moving funds from one account to another of the same type. For example, the act of moving funds from one IRA to another IRA or from one 403(b) to a second 403(b).

Transfer Upon Death account: A type of nonretirement account that has a named beneficiary who will receive the assets in the account upon the account owner's death.

Triggering event: A milestone that a participant experiences in order to become eligible to receive a distribution from a retirement plan.

University-sponsored retirement plan: A retirement plan established by a university employer that stipulates the conditions for participation by employees, such as vendor availability, annual contribution limit, and withdrawal restrictions.

Value fund: A mutual fund that favors buying stocks with lower price-to-earnings ratios and relatively high dividend yields, such as cyclical companies and companies found in mature industries.

Vendor: A company that participates in a university's retirement plan by accepting employer and employee contributions and offering various investment options to a participant.

Yield: The annual income return on an investment, expressed as a percentage of the price. For stocks, yield is the annual dividend divided by the current price, also known as a dividend yield. For bonds, it is the coupon rate divided by the market price, called current yield. For example, a bond selling for $1,000 with a 10 percent coupon ($100 coupon payment) offers a 10 percent current yield. If that bond's price rises to $1,500, the yield would fall to 6.7 percent for individuals that purchase at that higher price.